D0180820

WORKSHOP

METHODS OF WORK

The Best Tips from
25 Years of *Fine Woodworking*

WORKSHOP

METHODS OF WORK

EDITED AND
ILLUSTRATED BY
JIM RICHEY

The Taunton Press

Publisher: Jim Childs
Associate Publisher: Helen Albert
Associate Editor: Strother Purdy
Copy Editor: Diane Sinitsky
Indexer: Harriet Hodges
Art Director: Paula Schlosser
Cover and Interior Designer: Carol Singer
Layout Artist: Lisa DeFeo
Illustrator: Jim Richey

FINE WOODWORKING MAGAZINE
Editor: Timothy D. Schreiner
Art Director: Bob Goodfellow
Managing Editor: Anatole Burkin
Associate Editors: William Duckworth, Matthew
   Teague, Asa Christiana
Copy/Production Editor: Thomas McKenna
Associate Art Director: Michael Pekovich

ABOUT YOUR SAFETY
Working with wood is inherently dangerous. Using hand or power tools improperly or ignoring standard safety practices can lead to permanent injury or even death. Don't try to perform operations you learn about here (or elsewhere) unless you're certain they are safe for you. If something about an operation doesn't feel right, don't do it. Look for another way. We want you to enjoy the craft, so please keep safety foremost in your mind whenever you're working with wood.

Taunton
BOOKS & VIDEOS

for fellow enthusiasts

Text ©2000 by The Taunton Press, Inc.
Illustrations ©2000 by The Taunton Press, Inc.

All rights reserved.

Printed in the United States of America
10 9 8 7 6 5 4 3 2 1

The Taunton Press, Inc., 63 South Main Street, PO Box 5506,
Newtown, CT 06470-5506
e-mail: tp@taunton.com

Distributed by Publishers Group West

Library of Congress Cataloging-in-Publication Data
Workshop : methods of work / edited and illustrated by Jim Richey.
      p.   cm.
   "The best tips from 25 years of Fine woodworking."
   ISBN 1-56158-365-0
      1. Woodwork. I. Richey, Jim. II. Fine woodworking.
   TT180.W696   2000
   684'.08—dc21   00-044324

ACKNOWLEDGMENTS

MAKING GOOD MAGAZINE COLUMNS and books is not a solitary endeavor—it requires collaboration of the finest kind. Twenty-some years ago John Kelsey took a chance on me—thanks, John. My deepest gratitude goes to the magazine staff members I've worked with over the years: Rick Mastelli, Jim Cummins, Jim Boesel, Alec Waters, and Bill Duckworth. These guys did most of the hard work and didn't get much of the credit. I'd like also to recognize art directors Roland Wolf and Bob Goodfellow for their gentle and perceptive coaching. I am also most grateful for Strother Purdy's help and support in putting together this series of books.

But most important, I would like to thank the hundreds of woodworkers whose creative ideas and clever tricks are represented here. We couldn't have done it without you.

CONTENTS

INTRODUCTION

 AT MY HOUSE MY SHOP is my sanctuary, my little kingdom, the place I go to unwind and tinker. It is where I go to fix a broken lamp cord, sharpen the hoe, or make a wedding present for my daughter. Unlike the rest of my house, I can leave it messy or clean, put away my tools or not.

I think most of us feel this way about our shop—a refuge with sawdust on the floor. And over the years shops evolve and organically fit themselves around the personalities of the people who work in them and the problems they face. The layout of the tools will adapt to the space on hand and the sizes and types of projects. Clever little storage solutions will evolve to hold bits, bolts, and bandsaw blades. Jigs and patterns from past projects will decorate the walls. Racks will appear to hold wood and to hold clamps.

And every once in a while we have a clever idea, a solution to a long-standing shop problem that makes us smile. It might be a rolling stand for a table saw, or a storage bin for nuts and bolts, or a cut-off jig for a circular saw. It is these clever ideas that this book is about. We have selected the best of 25 years' worth of shop tips from *Fine Woodworking* magazine's Methods of Work and Q&A columns and collected them in this book. Here you will find ideas for clamping, measuring and marking, sanding, gluing, and sharpening. You will find clever fixtures of every variety.

So if your shop is your sanctuary, here are lots of ways to make it an even more interesting and effective place.

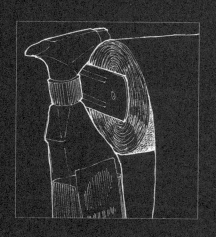

Chapter 1

SHOP SETUP

Rack for Clamping Pipes

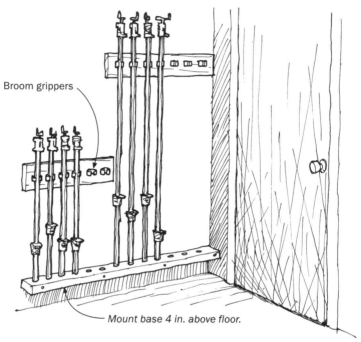

Broom grippers

Mount base 4 in. above floor.

S INCE I NORMALLY OVERCOMPLICATE things, I surprised myself
when I came up with this simple and effective pipe clamp rack
for ¾-in. iron pipe. It uses standard spring-metal broom grippers, the
kind you can find at most hardware stores, to hold the pipes. The
broom grippers are screwed to plywood strips that are in turn screwed
into wall studs. The base of the rack is a 2x4 with 1¼-in.-dia. holes
drilled halfway through to hold the ends of the pipes. Use drywall
screws to mount this base to studs 4 in. off the floor so you can sweep
under it. If you have a wide range of clamp lengths, as I do, you may
need two or more tiers of grippers. I installed the unit behind a door
to make effective use of the narrow space.

—KEVIN STAMM, *San Francisco, Calif.*

Quick-Grip Clamp Bracket

E VERYONE I HAVE TALKED with loves American Tool Companies'
Quick-Grip clamps, but they are awkward to hang. Here's a
simple hanger bracket that efficiently stores them. Using a couple
of side-by-side sawcuts, dado a groove just over ¼ in. wide and as
deep, about ¾ in. from the edge of a board. Then cut slots, again just
wider than ¼ in., into the board every couple of inches or so. Mount
the board on the wall or under the end of your workbench, and
hang the clamps in the slots by the little compression pins in the ends
of the bars.

—LLOYD W. WOOD, *Virginia Beach, Va.*

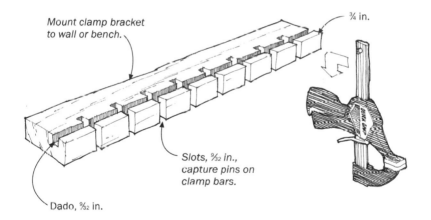

Mount clamp bracket
to wall or bench.

¾ in.

Slots, ⁹⁄₃₂ in.,
capture pins on
clamp bars.

Dado, ⁹⁄₃₂ in.

Cleat-System Shop Organizer

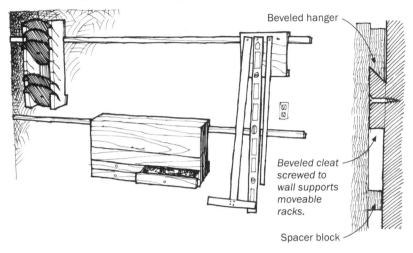

Beveled hanger

Beveled cleat screwed to wall supports moveable racks.

Spacer block

B EING A COMPULSIVE ORGANIZER, I have moved things around in my shop many times and I anticipate more moves in the future. To accommodate all this rearranging, I have come up with a cleat system that makes practically everything in my shop portable. The system consists of two beveled cleats attached to the shop walls. One cleat is attached 40 in. from the floor, a good working height, and the other at 64 in., a good hanging height. Any item I want to attach to the wall is fitted with a reverse-bevel hanger, as shown in the drawing. I use the system to hang my toolbox, router box, and drill box, to fasten a grinder to the wall, to position my work lights, and to attach hooks for rules and brooms. I use the cleats to hang everything that can be used in several locations in the shop. Later, I plan to build an identical cleat system inside a panel truck so I can transfer equipment between shop and truck quickly and neatly.

—JOHN LOUGHREY, Madison, Wisc.

Lumber Storage System

M Y BOSS, JIM GIBSON, was once a shipwright in his native Scotland. So when I asked him to help me design a lumber storage system for my basement shop, he had more than a few good ideas. This design for an adjustable storage rack, for example, has proved to be quite effective and inexpensive.

—DUANE F. HOLMES, *Ont., Canada*

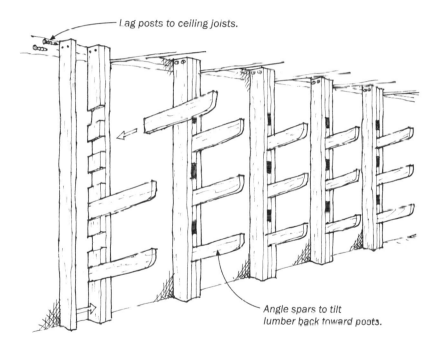

Lag posts to ceiling joists.

Angle spars to tilt lumber back toward posts.

Two Plywood Dollies

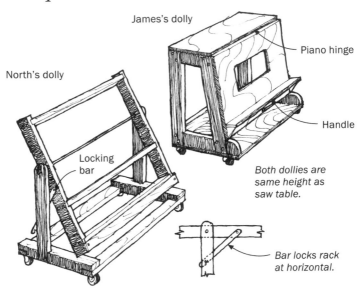

James's dolly

North's dolly

Piano hinge

Locking bar

Handle

Both dollies are same height as saw table.

Bar locks rack at horizontal.

FOR YEARS, I'VE BEEN using the dolly shown at right in the drawing to handle large, heavy panels. I use it to tilt the panels up to the top of my table saw and to unload panels from my truck. It also serves as a roll-around stepladder and a portable work surface.

—BEN JAMES, *Jacksonville, Fla.*

STRUGGLING WITH SHEETS OF plywood is a real strain on my back, so I built the plywood dolly shown at left in the drawing above to make handling the sheets easy. When I bring plywood to the shop in my pickup truck, I wheel the dolly up to the back of the truck with the cradle locked in the horizontal position. Then I slide the plywood from the truck onto the dolly with the long edge of the sheet resting against the foot. To transport, I tilt the cradle by tapping the locking bar with my foot, allowing it to swing to the vertical position.

When loaded with plywood, the cradle is almost evenly balanced but with a little more weight on the side with the foot so that it always tips the right way. After wheeling the plywood up to the saw, I tilt the cradle back to the horizontal position where the locking bar falls into a notch and locks. Since the dolly is the same height as my saw, I can feed the plywood directly into the saw from the dolly.

—R.W. NORTH, *Burbank, Calif.*

Plywood Keeper

I'VE USED THIS METHOD on stacks of plywood up to 30 sheets thick. Sink two eyescrews into the wall about 51 in. off the floor. Tie two sash weights to a piece of string and suspend each weight from an eyescrew. Cover the weights with foam pipe insulation to keep them from marring the plywood.

—JOHN R. THIESEN, *Cheektowaga, N.Y.*

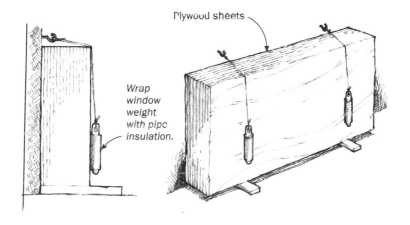

Plywood sheets

Wrap
window
weight
with pipe
insulation.

Hardware Storage Rack

Muffin tins fit slots
cut in box.

IN OUR ANTIQUE-AUTO RESTORATION shop we need a large inventory of standard screws, nuts, bolts, and washers in a variety of sizes. When we finally got tired of messing with those flimsy metal cabinets with the little plastic drawers, we built this rack for storing hardware in muffin tins. The rack itself is a simple box with grooves cut into the sides; you could build it any way you want. The main advantages of our setup are compactness, sturdiness, visibility of hardware (when the drawer is pulled out), and number of bins. Our rack uses 12 muffin tins, each with 12 compartments, giving us an ample 144 bins per unit. The muffin tins retail for around $4, so it is worth watching for a sale or scouting up a wholesale price.

—DURWARD BROWN AND WALLACE WIEBE, *Alva, Okla.*

Wall-Mounted Handsaw Hanger

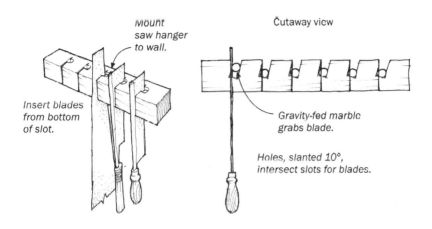

Mount saw hanger to wall.

Cutaway view

Insert blades from bottom of slot.

Gravity-fed marble grabs blade.

Holes, slanted 10°, intersect slots for blades.

THIS DEVICE WILL PROVIDE neat, secure storage for your handsaws, which normally are cumbersome to hang on the wall. Start with a 2x2 block of wood. Cut equally spaced 1½-in.-deep slots, one for each saw you want to store, and buy enough marbles so that you have one for each slot. Now drill a hole beside each slot, slightly angled, so each hole intersects a slot. These holes should be 1 in. deep and just a bit larger in diameter than the marble. Attach the hanger on the wall of your shop, so the holes are on top, and place a marble in each hole. Slide your saws up through the bottom of the slots, which will push the marbles up. Gravity will pull the marbles down to pinch against the blade and hold it in place.

—ROBERT ANDREWS, *San Diego, Calif.*

Hanging Tools with a Toggle

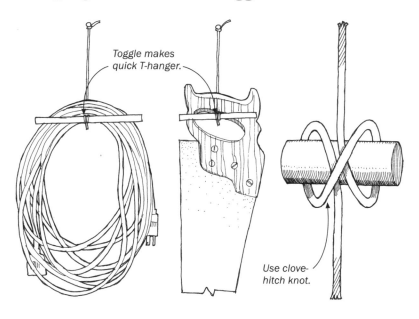

Toggle makes quick T-hanger.

Use clove-hitch knot.

T HIS SIMPLE HANGING SYSTEM, used by seamen to hang rope lines in lockers, is handy in the woodshop. Using a clove hitch, tie a short length of cord to a dowel and fasten the cord to the wall with a nail or screw eye. To use, pass the tethered dowel, called a toggle, through the handle of the tool. Various sized toggles can be used for different tools. This system works especially well for handsaws and coiled extension cords.

—SHERWOOD SCHWARTZ, *Palm Harbor, Fla.*

Making a Shop Moisture Gauge

THE DRAWING BELOW SHOWS a simple gauge you can make to give you a general idea of the relative humidity in your shop. The gauge will graphically show your customers how wood moves and why you build the way you do. For the gauge to work properly, the 20-in. wooden expansion arm must be sliced off the end of a wide panel or glued up from flatsawn segments, as shown. Movement of the gauge will be more dramatic if you pick a wood species that has a large tangential shrinkage percentage, such as beech, sugar maple, or white oak. If you have access to a moisture meter, you can scale the gauge numerically.

—JOHN SILLICK, Gasport, N.Y.

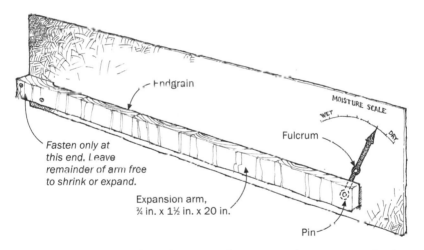

Endgrain

MOISTURE SCALE

WET

DRY

Fulcrum

Fasten only at
this end. Leave
remainder of arm free
to shrink or expand.

Expansion arm,
¾ in. x 1½ in. x 20 in.

Pin

Editor's Note: For formulas on predicting wood movement, check Bruce Hoadley's book *Understanding Wood* (The Taunton Press, 63 S. Main St., Newtown, CT 06470).

Eye-Protection Cleaning Station

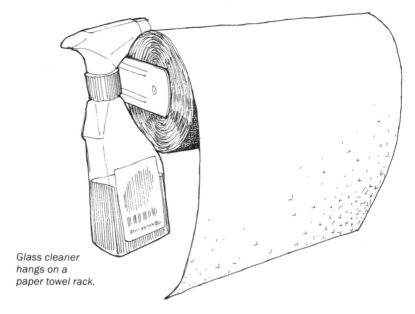

Glass cleaner
hangs on a
paper towel rack.

N O ONE IN MY SHOP likes to wear eye protection. Glasses and goggles get fogged up and scratched, and they attract dust like magnets. But after having debris surgically removed from my left cornea, we all got serious about eye protection. Now we hang a bottle of glass cleaner on a paper-towel dispenser to make an eye-protection cleaning station. The ammonia in the glass cleaner seems to repel dust and keep the lenses from fogging up.

—CHRIS BLACK, *Clifton, Va.*

Setting Up a Dust-Collection System

TO SET UP A DUST-COLLECTION system using a cyclone separator and tube filters, the first step is to determine the amount of air required by each machine to take care of the wood dust generated. In a small, typical woodshop, it is most likely that you will be running only one machine at a time. Therefore, you should determine the size of your dust-collection system according to the air requirements of your largest machine. This is usually the planer, which can require up to a 900-cubic-feet-per-minute (CFM) blower capacity. In this case, a 2-hp/1,000 CFM system would probably be best. For a 2-hp unit, with air usage between 800 and 1,200 CFM, the pipe should be sized to maintain a conveying velocity between 3,500 to 4,500 feet per minute.

The dust/air mixture travels through the system in the following manner: It is first collected at the machine and then conveyed to the cyclone where all but the finest particles are separated from the air. The fine dust/air mix then moves through the fan and on to the filter bags.

The heart of the dust system will run approximately $200 for a cyclone, $350 for a 2-hp dust collector (includes motor and blower), and about $150 for a set of tube filters. Finally, there's the cost of the duct work, collection hoods, and plywood that is required to put the new, improved system together.

The complete system does not have to be set up all in one place. The cyclone and fan could be put outside the shop and the bag filters inside. This would move the noise of the system outside yet return heated or cooled air to the shop. However, adding the cyclone and extra filters will reduce the noise level of the system.

Explosions are unlikely in either the cyclone or the tube filters if these components are sized appropriately for the system. Separation of dust and air in a cyclone occurs rapidly, and the air-to-dust ratio is not high enough to allow for an explosion or fire. Because of the high pre-separation in the cyclone, little dust gets to the tube filters, and even if there were enough dust, the filters cannot contain an explosion. Static sparks are generally not a factor because the blower motor is statically grounded. The cyclone would also be grounded if it's connected to the blower by metal ducting. Any plastic ducting should be grounded by running a bare copper wire inside the duct.

Blowers with aluminum fan wheels are recommended for woodshops because aluminum is a non-ferrous material, which cannot transmit sparks. Nevertheless, a fire could occur if the wood-dust material is not removed and a high concentration of dust builds up in the bags. Then a static spark from improperly grounded plastic pipe or some other source could ignite the dust.

—PETER FEDRIGON, *Cleveland, N.Y.,*
from a question by Gary Gilbert, Somerville, Mass.

Sizing a Dust-Collection System

R ECENTLY I CONSULTED WITH a woodworker who was adding a dust-collection system to his shop. He wanted to run 26 ft. of 2½-in.-dia. tubing to collect the dust and wondered how powerful a collector he would need. I told him that, first of all, his plan of running 26 ft. of 2½-in. tubing would not work. He would need to use an extremely high-powered blower (the fan of the central collector) to move the volume of air required to convey the dust generated by a tablesaw, jointer, planer, or shaper. Though it's beyond the scope of this explanation to go into all the factors and formulas needed to properly design a dust-collection system, here's a basic rundown on the relationship of duct diameter to air volume, velocity, and friction losses that occur as air travels through a duct.

Dust collectors are rated by the volume of air they can move (measured in cubic feet per minute, or cfm) while overcoming the friction of the airflow in the duct work and in the blower itself (stated as static pressure, or sp, measured in inches of water). Therefore, a collector that is rated to move 1,200 cfm with no friction (0 sp loss) might only manage 100 cfm or so when the friction's up to, say, 8 in. of sp loss.

Now, given the same collector hooked up to two different-diameter ducts, the air would flow faster through the smaller one. This is because air velocity increases as duct diameter decreases—think of how much faster a stream of water flows as it passes through a narrow garden-hose nozzle. If you want to move a large volume of air through a small-diameter duct, the air would have to travel at a very high speed. In your situation, to move the amount of air required to collect the dust from an average tablesaw (350 cfm is typical), the air would have to travel at around 9,000 feet per minute, or fpm. This is more than double what is normally recommended for woodworking dust-collection systems, which is 3,500 fpm for main ducts and 4,000 fpm for branch ducts.

The reason that the air would have to travel so fast is that it would have to overcome a huge static pressure loss (lots of friction). Static-pressure losses increase as the diameter of duct decreases. And sp losses are cumulative over distance: the longer the duct (and the more bends and junctures it has), the greater the friction and, therefore, the higher the sp losses.

The higher the total sp losses in a duct system, the more powerful the collector must be to overcome them. In the original scenario, the woodworker would have 0.72 in. sp loss per foot. Over 26 ft. of straight duct (no elbows or turns), this would amount to a whopping 18.72 in. of sp loss—enough to choke even a huge collector. By way of comparison, a heavy-duty, 3-hp collector can handle only about 9 in. of sp loss when moving 400 cfm (about what you'd need for a shaper and less than is recommended for a bandsaw).

I told the woodworker to stick with a typical small-shop dust collector and connect it to his machines with large-diameter ductwork. A 5-in. main line with 4-in. branch lines should be about right. These ducts are large enough to carry the volume of air and chips from most shop machines while maintaining recommended air velocities. And for the relatively short 26-ft. run he is planning, I'd guess a 2-hp unit should be able to handle the modest friction losses in the 4-in.- and 5-in.-dia. ducts.

—SANDOR NAGYSZALANCZY, *Santa Cruz, Calif.,*
from a question by Ted Baca, Evans, Colo.

Simplified Dust-Collector Switch

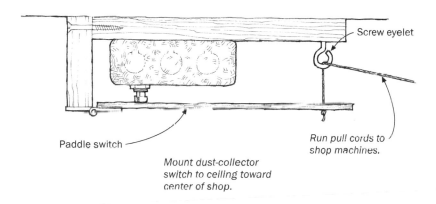

Screw eyelet

Paddle switch

Run pull cords to shop machines.

Mount dust-collector switch to ceiling toward center of shop.

O VER THE YEARS, I HAVE seen several designs in *Fine Woodworking* for switching a dust-collection system on and off. All seemed too complicated or impractical for my situation.

My alternative is a simple mechanical system using a cord, much like what is used on a city bus to signal the driver for a desired stop. I located the switch box at a convenient central location on the ceiling of my shop. Then, by running several cords to different areas of the shop, I am able to turn the dust collector on or off simply by reaching up and pulling the cord from whatever machine I am using.

– KIM ANDERSON, *Loyalton, Calif.*

Remote Control
for Dust-Collection System

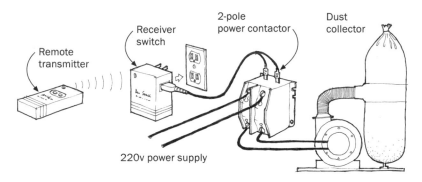

Remote transmitter

Receiver switch

2-pole power contactor

Dust collector

220v power supply

RECENTLY, I MOVED MY CUSTOM woodworking business out of my home into a historic mill. As part of the move, I made several shop improvements, including upgrading to a 2-hp dust-collection system that I hooked up to several additional tools. That's when the problem surfaced. I was spending too much time running over to the dust-collector switch.

One evening, I plunked down my weary bones, grabbed the remote, and turned on the television. Click. I realized my dust-collector problems were over. I purchased a remote-activated on/off switch from Radio Shack for less than $25, which works like a television remote. By itself, the Radio Shack switch is not beefy enough to power the collection system's motor, so I bought a 2-pole, 30-amp/240v AC contactor with a 110v AC coil and enclosure from my local electrical supply distributor for about $60. The Radio Shack remote-controlled switch serves as a pilot for the heavy-duty contactor.

After a couple of hours of wiring, I could start or stop my collector from any location in the shop, which is a real time-saver when a customer walks in or the phone rings.

—JEROME LOUISON, *Savage, Md.*

Flexible Duct Solves Awkward Dust Hookups

M Y DUST COLLECTOR IS mounted on a dolly, which can be rolled around the shop and hooked up to whichever machine I'm using. Flexible hose works well in this situation. I use flexible aluminum ducting, made by Dundas Jafine (available through your local building supply dealer), which is spiral-wound from corrugated aluminum. The ducting comes in diameters from 3 in. to 14 in. Besides being flexible, it is much more durable than plastic film-over-wire drier duct. It also doesn't collapse under suction and is easy to cut to length.

Some flow capacity is lost because of the rough texture of this material, so I wouldn't run ductwork for an entire shop from this product. But wherever you have a portable collector or need severe bends, it's ideal.

—GUY LAUTARD, *West Vancouver, B.C., Canada*

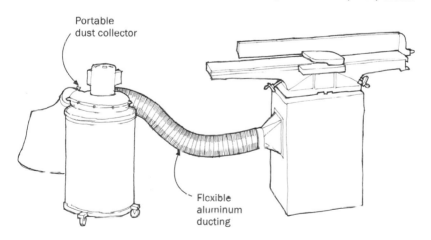

Portable
dust collector

Flexible
aluminum
ducting

Squirrel-Cage Fan and Dust Filter

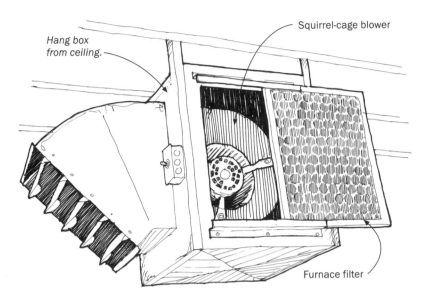

Hang box from ceiling.

Squirrel-cage blower

Furnace filter

I WAS CONCERNED ABOUT DUST in my shop and had this filter setup made at a sheet-metal shop. For about $140, I got the four-speed squirrel-cage blower in a custom box with a furnace filter on each side. It hangs on the ceiling where it filters the air by removing air-borne dust before it settles. It then recirculates the filtered air with a whirlpool effect.

—JOHN R. THIESEN, *South Wales, N.Y.*

Hose Clamps to the Rescue

A FTER SEVERAL MISHAPS WITH the bag coming off my dust collector, I made up a new band with a hose clamp, as shown. Start
with a 4-in. hose clamp. Cut it in two about midway, and pop-rivet a
length of steel or plastic band (the kind used to secure shipping car-
tons) between the two ends to lengthen the clamp to whatever size
you need.

—RAY NAMIOTKA, *Pittsburgh, Pa.*

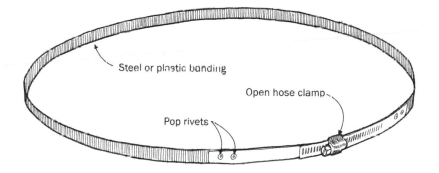

Steel or plastic banding

Open hose clamp

Pop rivets

Portable Flood Lights

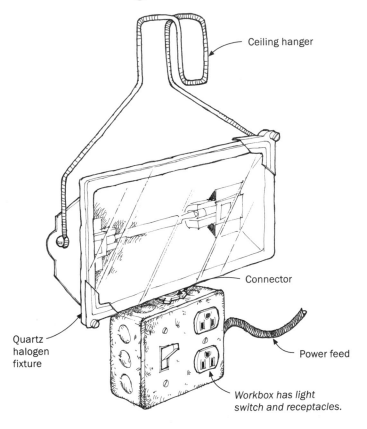

Ceiling hanger

Connector

Quartz halogen fixture

Power feed

Workbox has light switch and receptacles.

FOR THESE PORTABLE FLOOD lights in my shop, I placed a connection box below the lamp and then added a long, heavy steel-wire hook to hang the unit 10 in. to 12 in. from the ceiling. This arrangement minimizes heat buildup in the circuit box. I also chose to use a larger 4-in. electrical box so that I could switch the light and power outlet on and off.

—JIM ALLEN, *Atlanta, Ga.*

Shop Wiring: 110v vs. 220v

M ANY WOODWORKERS ARE CONFUSED about when to run 110v and when to run 220v wiring in the shop. First, let's dispel the myth about operating motors on various voltages: An electric motor operating on 110/115v will use the same amount of power (to do the same amount of work) as it does on 220/230v. (A few definitions will help here: A watt is a measure of electrical power; a volt denotes potential differences that cause the current to flow; and an ampere is a measure of the amount of current flowing through a wire.) The myth that the motor will use less power on the higher voltage comes from the fact that it uses half as many amperes (amps) on the higher voltage. But what you buy from your utility is watts, not amps. The number of watts equals the number of amps times the number of volts. Thus, when the amps are half but the volts are double, the watts will be the same.

The advantage of using 230v for heavier machinery is that you can run slightly smaller wires to the machines because the full-load amps will be one-half of the 115v value. Because of the lower amp load, the line voltage drop at the machine under heavy cutting conditions will be less. With more stable voltage, the motor will develop higher torque than it would under sagging or low-voltage conditions, which can occur if the motor is operated at the lower voltage.

In general, motors up through 1 hp can be operated quite successfully on 115v. Operating on 115v gives greater portability because this voltage is commonly available in any shop or job site. Machines with 2-hp and larger motors will operate better on 230v. Motors with 1½ hp can operate successfully at either 115v or 230v.

—EDWARD COWERN, *Wallingford, Conn.,*
from a question by Al Coppola, Mulvane, Kan.

Overhead Plug-Ins

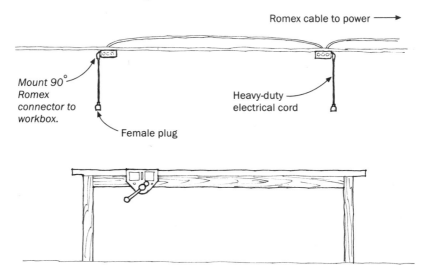

Romex cable to power ⟶

Mount 90°
Romex
connector to
workbox.

Female plug

Heavy-duty
electrical cord

T HIS SIMPLE BIT OF REWIRING solves the problem of having a cord underfoot when using routers, drills, and the like at your workbench. Run Romex cable above the ceiling, mount workboxes to joists, and with 90° Romex connectors, drop heavy rubber-covered electrical cord with a female plug. A rubber band or twist tie will keep a long tool cord overhead and out of the way when not in use.

—ERIC L. MYNTER, *Remsen, N.Y.*

Lighting a Woodworking Shop

TO LIGHT A TYPICAL GARAGE woodworking shop (a room 20 ft. by 18 ft. with small windows on three sides, for example), you will need 16 dual 40-watt fluorescent fixtures suspended at approximately 8 ft. high to produce the necessary 15-ft.-candle intensity at benchtop height. The fixtures should be equipped with opaque reflectors so that the lighting will be direct. Diffusers are not needed.

The fixtures should be arranged in four rows of four fixtures each with even spacing. Rows 1 and 3 should be on one switch-activated circuit, and rows 2 and 4 should be on a second circuit, for economical daytime operation when the sunlight is intense. However, many shops are most frequently used at night, so windows are not considered in intensity calculations. Local lighting of machines such as drill presses, jigsaws, and lathes is always desirable.

— DR. ROBERT BROWN,
from a question by Stewart Wurtz, New Gloucester, Maine

Problems of an Aging Motor

W HEN AN AGING SINGLE-PHASE motor seems to be starting slowly, there are two common points of failure to examine. One is the starting switch and the other is the starting capacitor.

The starting switch is usually a centrifugal device built to snap open and switch off the starting circuit when the motor reaches approximately three-quarters of its full speed. This switch usually has weights and springs, like a fly-ball governor seen on old steam engines in museums. Frequently, in woodworking shops, the moving components of the switch get fouled with sawdust or pitch and become stuck or operate sluggishly. If the switch sticks in the open position, the motor will hum but not start; if it gets stuck in the closed position, the motor will be quite noisy and if left on, it will get very hot and possibly fail. Starting-switch problems can be prevented by keeping motors clean and blowing away accumulated sawdust before it gets into the motor. In a very dusty shop, it might be a good idea to switch to a TEFC (totally enclosed, fan-cooled) motor.

The second failure point on single-phase motors is the starting capacitor—this is a black plastic cylinder usually mounted externally (in some cases, it's mounted inside the motor). Occasionally, the capacitor will weaken or short out. When the capacitor weakens, the motor becomes slow starting. If the capacitor shorts, the motor will be very noisy, may start or run slowly, and exhibit the same symptoms as if the starting switch is stuck in the closed position. When it fails completely, the motor hums but doesn't start just as in the case of a starting switch that's stuck open.

It is relatively easy to replace a bad capacitor if it's externally mounted. It is more difficult to replace an internal capacitor or to replace a bad starter switch, but these jobs are still within the capability of most people who are handy. Always make sure the motor is fully disconnected from the power system before attempting any repair. Replacement parts are available through most electric-motor service shops. The value of the motor's capacitor is usually stamped on the capacitor and is given in terms of microfarads (mfd) and operating voltage, such as 125 volts or AC.

—EDWARD COWERN, *Wallingford, Conn.,*
from a question by Nathan James, Colorado Springs, Colo.

Variable-Speed Control
for Universal Motors

M ANY WOODWORKERS HESITATE TO use variable-speed controls
with their tools because they have heard that these devices
work fine with some motors but may damage other motors. Here's a
simple primer.

The variable-speed controls offered by several manufacturers,
including MLCS, Penn State Industries, and Lutron, are really adjustable voltage controls and work very much like transformers used for
electric trains. One exception is that the electronics in these devices
can sense motor load that regulates the speed of the power tool to
maintain a nearly constant speed, during both light- and heavy-duty
work loads. This is highly desirable on tools that must handle variable
loading, such as portable drills and routers.

Speed control units always carry the disclaimer that they may only
be used with tools powered by universal AC/DC motors. The feature
that distinguishes a universal from other motor types is the use of
brushes. Motors with brushes are easy to spot: Two removable caps
that cover the brush assemblies can usually be seen on either side of
the motor housing. With the exception of battery-powered tools,
almost any portable power tool (and some small stationary machines)
equipped with brushes has a universal motor and can be used with a
variable-speed control. AC motors used on most stationary power
tools sport induction motors. Their speed cannot be controlled by
voltage but is instead fixed by the frequency of the power.

While in most cases the results of using a variable-speed controller with a portable power tool will be good, occasionally, due to the peculiarities of some motors, the motor speed may fluctuate instead of remaining stable. But you can rest assured that in either case, no harm will be done to the motor or the tool.

—EDWARD COWERN, *Wallingford, Conn.,*
from a question by David Carlson, Richland, Wash.

Reversing Belt-Driven Tools

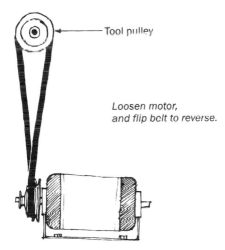

Tool pulley

Loosen motor,
and flip belt to reverse.

I T'S EASY TO REVERSE DISC sanders and other belt-driven tools if the motor is mounted perpendicular to the shaft it drives, so there's a quarter-turn in the belt, as shown. To reverse, simply loosen the belt, flip 180° (on either pulley), and tighten. An added advantage is that the twist in the belt seems to dampen vibrations.

—ROGER LYNNE, *Bloomington, Minn.*

Reducing an Electric Motor's Speed for Buffing

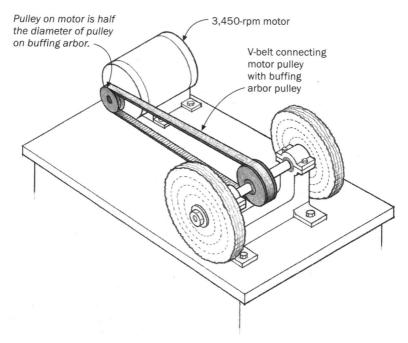

Pulley on motor is half the diameter of pulley on buffing arbor.

3,450-rpm motor

V-belt connecting motor pulley with buffing arbor pulley

S OME WOODWORKERS LIKE TO finish small projects by buffing the wood. But a 3,450-rpm motor turning a buffing wheel runs too fast and will burn the wood. The simplest and best way to reduce an electric motor's speed for buffing is to separate the motor and the buffing wheels, connecting them with a V-belt and pulleys of two different sizes.

To reduce the speed of a 3,450-rpm motor by half, use a pulley on the arbor that is twice the diameter of the motor pulley (see the drawing). Just as with bicycle gears, the small pulley on the motor will rotate twice for each rotation of the arbor pulley, reducing the speed of the larger pulley to 1,725 rpm. If you put several pulleys on the arbor shaft, you can vary the speed of the buffing wheels.

A ½-hp motor is plenty powerful for buffing. The most important factor, as you've already realized, is speed. Reducing the speed at the buffing wheels to 1,725 rpm should be sufficient to prevent the wood that you're buffing from being burned.

—GARY ROGOWSKI, *Portland, Ore.,*
from a question by Edward Jonke, Glen Arm, Md.

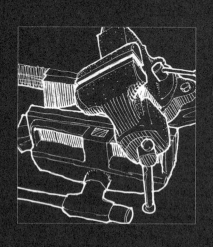

Chapter 2

WORKBENCHES, VISES & SAWHORSES

Inexpensive Bench Vise

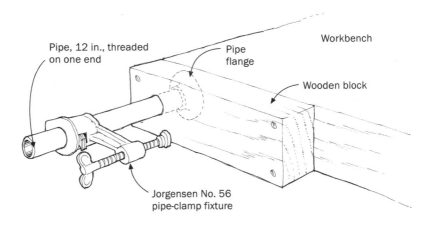

Pipe, 12 in., threaded on one end

Pipe flange

Workbench

Wooden block

Jorgensen No. 56 pipe-clamp fixture

T HIS INEXPENSIVE SUBSTITUTE FOR a left-handed workbench vise allows you to clamp a panel all the way to the floor, if necessary. It has no guide rods or screw to interfere with a vertical workpiece, as with a metal vise. It may not match the quality of a left-handed vise from a top-end woodworking bench, but it is surprisingly useful and easy to build.

To make the vise, first secure a pipe flange to the bench edge. Use long screws because the vise exerts a lot of pressure. Fit a 2-in.-thick block over the flange, as shown. Screw the block to the workbench. A 12-in. pipe threaded on one end and the movable end from a Jorgensen No. 56 clamp fixture complete the assembly. If desired, attach a wooden block to the end of the clamp screw pad to gain more surface area and to even out pressure. Take care not to walk into the pipe.

—ANTHONY GUIDICE, *St. Louis, Mo.*

Universal Vise

IT'S COMMON FOR WOODWORKERS to mount an engineer's vise on a block of wood so it can be clamped in a woodworking vise and used to hold a piece of metal. To extend the clamping range of the vise-in-a-vise concept, choose a small engineering vise with a pivoting base, and bolt it to a 2-in.-square hardwood post that extends about 5 in. beyond the vise. This allows you to vary the position of the post in the carpenter's vise to obtain an almost unlimited number of clamping angles.

—A. D. GOODE, *Sapphire, N.S.W., Australia*

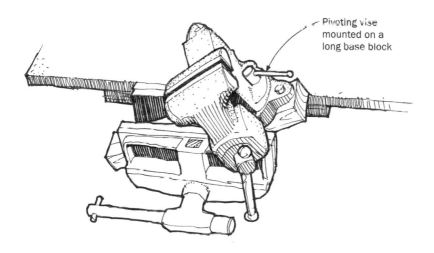

Pivoting vise mounted on a long base block

A Work Holder That Swivels

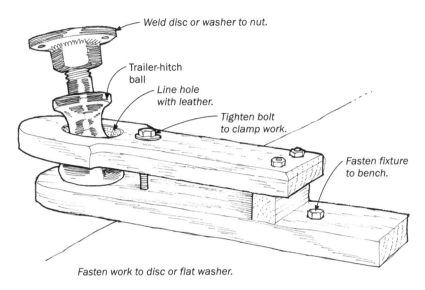

Weld disc or washer to nut.

Trailer-hitch ball

Line hole with leather.

Tighten bolt to clamp work.

Fasten fixture to bench.

Fasten work to disc or flat washer.

I RECENTLY NEEDED A SWIVEL-TYPE work holder—the kind carvers use. Because the price for a commercial holder was about $125, I decided to make my own with a trailer-hitch ball and some shop scraps, as shown. The fixture is simply two pieces of hardwood that lock the hitch ball in place when a bolt is tightened. Line the hole in the top board with leather so it will grip better. For the workpiece plate, weld a large washer or disc to the nut, or attach it with screws tapped into the holes in the nut.

—HARRY J. GURNEY, *Taunton, Mass.*

Horizontal Vise

T HIS HORIZONTAL VISE, INSTALLED on a workbench, is indispensable for sanding, routing, carving, and planing. For many operations it holds the work better than bench dogs. The vise consists of
three simple parts: a bench screw, an oak jaw, and a wooden step-
block. Mount the bench screw's nut to the bench from the bottom so
that the surface will be flat if you remove the vise. Cut the 2-in.-thick
jaw about 20 in. or so long. Drill an oversize hole in the jaw about
7 in. from the back and fasten the bench screw through the hole.
Bandsaw the step-block from a 4x4. Cut the steps taller one way than
the other so you can flip the block and use it both ways. To keep the
back end of the jaw from slipping off the sides of the step block, glue
a piece of plywood to each side.

—PENDLETON TOMPKINS, *San Mateo, Calif.*

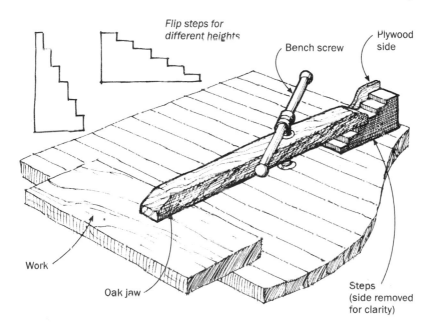

Flip steps for
different heights

Bench screw

Plywood
side

Work

Oak jaw

Steps
(side removed
for clarity)

Portable Vise

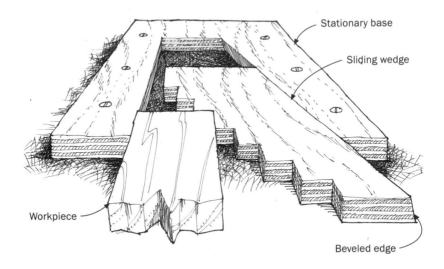

Stationary base

Sliding wedge

Workpiece

Beveled edge

A S A YOUNGSTER, SOME 60 years ago, I often watched my father doing finish work using a light workbench, which he hauled from job to job. One of the attachments on that bench was a shop-made wooden vise, like the one shown in the drawing. I reproduced the vise from memory and find it a versatile aid for holding stock both on edge for planing or flat for scraping.

To make the vise, I selected a scrap rectangle of ¾-in. birch plywood, cut the sliding wedge from it with a beveled edge on the angled side, then notched the other side of the wedge at ½-in. intervals. I fasten work in the vise by finding the notch that fits and then tapping the wedge tightly into the jaws. A quick tap on the other end of the sliding wedge will loosen the workpiece. If I were making another, I would use ⅝-in. material so ¾-in. stock would stand a bit proud of the vise and thus be easily dressed.

—ALFRED S. WHITE, *Los Angeles, Calif.*

Folding Saw Rack

THIS MULTIPURPOSE FOLDING RACK takes the place of several sawhorses, yet when stored it occupies less space than one. Unfolded, it can support a 4x8 sheet of plywood for ripping or cross-cutting. It's also handy for cutting 2x4s to length and other framing work. With a piece of plywood on top, it becomes a handy work platform.

—PHIL MACKIE, *Rhinelander, Wisc.*

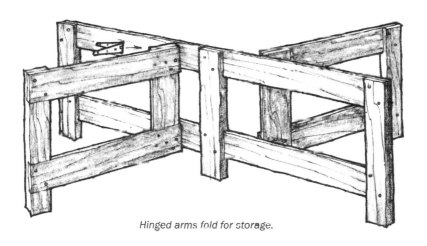

Hinged arms fold for storage.

A Basic Sawhorse

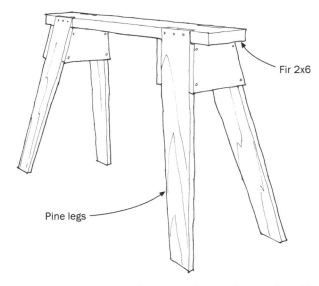

Fir 2x6

Pine legs

THIS BASIC DESIGN WILL produce a sawhorse that is adaptable to several workshop tasks, sturdy, good-looking, and a pride to own. To build a basic pair of sawhorses you'll need one 8-ft. 2x6, three 8-ft. 1x6s plus a few 1x6 scraps for braces. Fir or pine is the usual choice because of its strength and light weight. All operations in sawhorse construction can be performed with hand tools, but power tools make the job faster and easier.

Start by cutting two 42-in.-long pieces of 2x6 for the saddles. Some people prefer to use a saddle 48 in. long, but the 42-in. length is handier for working on doors and still gives plenty of support to a 4x8 sheet of plywood. Next cut eight legs 28 in. long from the 1x6 stock. Once the sawhorses are assembled, the legs will be trimmed to give an overall height of 24 in. Taper the legs on one edge, starting full width at a point 8 in. from the top and tapering down to 3½ in. at the bottom. This makes the horse lighter and more stable.

When the legs are done, cut the gains (notches) in the saddle to receive them. This is probably the most critical part of making sawhorses. The gains are cut on a compound angle, and much of the strength of the sawhorse depends on a good fit. Use a steel square to make the angles. Make the first mark 3½ in. from the end of the saddle. Place the square on the edge of the 2x6 so the 3-in. mark on one leg and the 12-in. mark on the other line up with the face corner of the 2x6, and scribe a 4:1 (75°) slope. Line up a 1x6 leg with this slope and use its opposite edge to make a second mark. This gives you the lengthwise slope of the leg. Now determine the spread of the legs across the width. There are two dimensions in common use. For a sawhorse used in house framing, the spread should be 14 in., as this allows it to be carried between studs that are on 16-in. centers. A 20-in. spread is better for finish work and shop use because of the added stability.

Mark the gains for this angle on top of the 2x6 by scribing a line ¾ in. in from the edge between the two marks previously made. On the bottom make a line that will vary according to the spread you choose. For the 14-in. spread, it should be ½ in. in from the edge; for the 20-in. spread, ⅜ in.

Using a handsaw, cut along the marks on the edge of the 2x6. Stop cutting when the teeth touch the lines on the top and bottom of the 2x6. Now make parallel sawcuts about ½ in. apart between the first two cuts, stopping at the top and bottom lines also. Use a chisel to clean out the gain. Cut the leg braces from the leftover pieces of 1x6.

Hold a piece in position and mark the angles of the legs on it, making sure the legs are spread to the correct degree and the angles are equal. Use this as a pattern to cut the rest of the braces. Bevel the top of each brace so it will fit flush under the saddle. After the braces have been fastened with glue and nails, trim the legs flush with the top of the saddle using a handsaw.

With the horse standing on a flat surface, measure the distance from the top of the saddle to the ground. Set a scriber for the difference between this measurement and 24 in. Scribe around each leg to get a cutting line that will allow the legs to sit flat. Chamfer and sand all the corners and edges to avoid possible slivers and cuts, then finish with oil.

—SAM ALLEN, *Provo, Utah*

Frame-and-Foot Sawhorses

FOR A SAWHORSE THAT is useful in supporting cabinets and carcases as you work, laying out cuts in long boards, or for various other jobs around the shop, here's one (basically a frame on two feet) that is light and strong, yet stores easily without taking up a lot of space. I made mine out of red oak (because I had a large quantity on hand), but you can make them out of almost any wood you choose.

All the pieces are ¹⁵⁄₁₆ in. thick and 2½ in. wide, except for the foot, which is 1¾₁₆ in. wide. The uprights are through-tenoned into the feet and secured with glue and a couple of ¼-in. pegs. To receive the stretcher, I chopped through-mortises in the uprights. The tenons, which I cut long to use the same saw setting, were trimmed to length after assembly. They are also pinned with ¼-in. dowels, though wedges would do as well. Both uprights and the saddle member are notched to make a secure double-lap joint, which can be pinned or not.

These horses can be made quickly and in quantity with a minimum of materials and fuss. I have a couple dozen of them. They travel well, taking up much less space than conventional four-leg horses, and they nestle together neatly when not in use.

—HANK GILPIN, *Lincoln, R.I.*

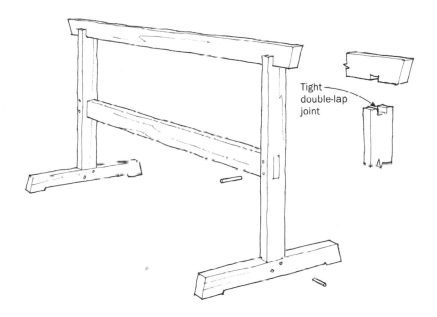

Tight double-lap joint

Knockdown Sawhorse

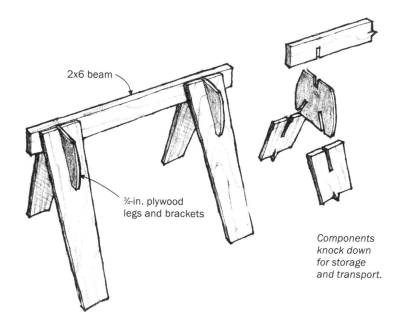

2x6 beam

¾-in. plywood
legs and brackets

*Components
knock down
for storage
and transport.*

HERE'S A SAWHORSE WITH no metal parts to mar your work. These horses stack neatly, and they can also be knocked apart easily for storage or transport. The plywood legs are 8 in. wide at the top, though 6 in. will work if you want to cut down on weight. The only caution is that the sliding joints must be cut tight enough so that they must be driven with a hammer, or the horse will wobble. This construction is much stronger than it looks at first glance—I've put one sawhorse through the teenage-student torture test in my shop class, where it survives unbroken.

—MARK BLIESKE, *Winnipeg, Man., Canada*

Sawing and Assembly Workstation

HERE'S A SHOP AID that let me put three different sets of saw-horses out to pasture. It makes a strong, portable workstation for sawing, sanding, assembly, and other operations. Simply flop the box to position the work 24 in., 30 in., or 36 in. off the floor, whichever is convenient. Construct the unit by screwing together six dowel-joined frames.

—BILL NOLAN, *Munising, Mich.*

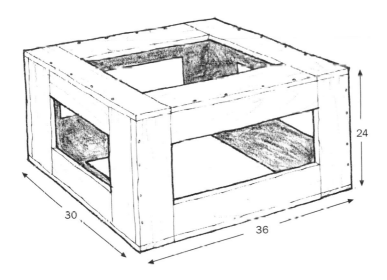

Two-Level Rolling Worktable

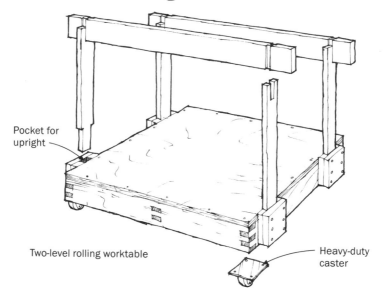

Pocket for upright

Two-level rolling worktable

Heavy-duty caster

I MADE THIS ROLLING WORKTABLE to ease the logistics of constructing a full set of kitchen cabinets in my small (18-ft. by 18-ft.) workshop. Since then I have found it to be the ideal companion to the traditional cabinetmaker's workbench when space is limited. Square, level, and strong, the base is excellent for moving cabinets and furniture. The device can be used as a waist-high movable worktable. As a bonus, it stores away without taking up much room.

Four 360° heavy-duty casters support a 40-in. by 40-in. finger-jointed or dovetailed frame of 2x3 hardwood, gusseted with ¾-in. plywood at each corner. Add a couple of 1x3 crossbraces if needed. Screw and glue the ¾-in. plywood top to the frame, then paint and wax it to make it easy to clean up spilled glue and finishes. Next add two pockets on each of two opposite sides, as shown, to accept the ends of the four hardwood 1x3 uprights. Slot the top of each upright to slip into the two appropriately notched crossbars. These four uprights and two crossbars can be assembled in about 30 seconds to produce a table-height workhorse.

—Norman Odell, *Quathiaski Cove, B.C., Canada*

Outdoor Workbench

I NEEDED A SMALL OUTDOOR bench for fair-weather work outside my shop and for demonstrations at the county fair. To make the bench I cut a beefy slice of oak tree and mounted it on three legs canted outward. For the "vise," I fitted the bench with holes for my cast-iron hold-down (available from Woodcraft, 560 Airport Industrial Park, Parkersburg, WV 26102-1686). I bored a 2-in. hole into the top of the bench clear through to the bottom (so rainwater wouldn't collect in the hole). Then I plugged the top 2 in. of the hole with hardwood and centerbored the plug to fit the hold-down shaft. I flattened a place on the side of the oak slice and fitted a plug as above so I could use the hold-down to clamp work vertically.

—J. B. Small, *Newville, Pa.*

SHOPMADE HAND TOOLS & HAND-TOOL FIXTURES

Dovetail Marking Setup

T HIS SETUP FOR SCRIBING pin sockets in hand-dovetail construction eliminates hand-held slipping and repositioning problems. Put a spacer block under a handscrew on the workbench. Align the two workpieces, tighten the handscrew, then lock the whole into position with a C-clamp.

—RICHARD KENDROT, *Windsor, N.Y.*

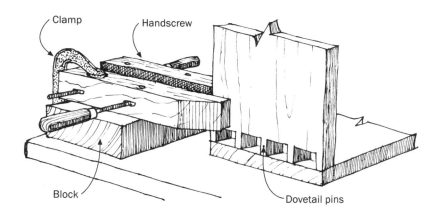

Clamp

Handscrew

Block

Dovetail pins

Shoulder Block for Hand-Cut Dovetails

THIS SIMPLE LITTLE SHOULDER block is not my idea, but I've adopted it and now have several different sizes for different situations. To make the block, start with two 1¼-in.-sq. sticks of hardwood, about 4 in. longer than the widest dovetail you normally cut. Drill through the ends and install carriage bolts and wing nuts, as shown in the sketch below.

To use the block after you've marked out the pins, carefully tighten the block on the workpiece at the base of the pins. The shoulder block serves two purposes: as a cutting-depth stop and as a chisel guide for removing the waste.

With the block in place, simply saw the pins until the blade touches the block. After sawing, clamp the block and workpiece in a wood-faced vise, lay the chisel's flat side against the block, and begin tapping away the waste. The block will guide the chisel up to the line. This shoulder block is also useful for paring the shoulders of tenons and cleaning up through-mortises.

–LEN CRANE, BASIN VIEW, N.S.W., Australia

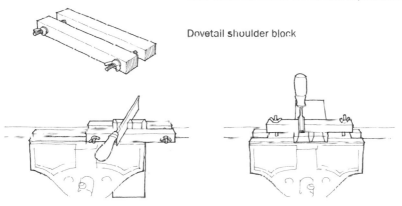

Dovetail shoulder block

The block serves as a cutting-depth stop
and as a guide for the flat of a chisel.

Marking Dovetail Pins

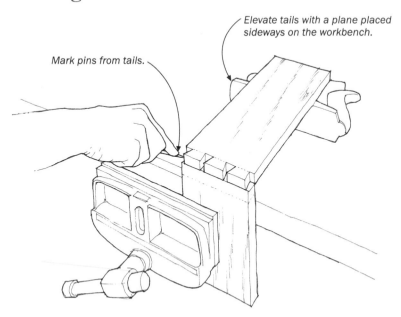

Elevate tails with a plane placed sideways on the workbench.

Mark pins from tails.

HERE'S A TRICK THAT SIMPLIFIES the critical step of marking dovetails. Cut the tails in the drawer side first. Lay a handplane on its side on the bench, and clamp the drawer front (on which the pins will be marked) in the vise to the height of the plane. It's easy to lay the drawer side across the plane body and the clamped drawer front and then transfer the outline of the tails to the pins by marking them with a knife or an awl.

—ANTHONY GUIDICE, *St. Louis, Mo.*

Modified Dovetail Saw Works on the Pull Stroke

T AKE AN ORDINARY FINE-TOOTHED dovetail saw, and clamp it in a
vise close to its spine. Gently tap the handle up to remove the
blade. Then reverse the handle, so the blade cuts on the pull stroke. Tap
the spine back on the blade, and clamp the spine between the vise jaws.
Sharpen as usual, but with little or no set. The result is not an authentic
Japanese saw, but it is similar to a Chinese coffin-maker's saw and a lot
easier to sharpen.

—JOE SANTAPAU, *Yardley, Pa.*

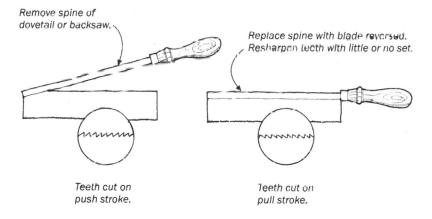

Remove spine of
dovetail or backsaw.

Replace spine with blade reversed.
Resharpen teeth with little or no set.

Teeth cut on
push stroke.

Teeth cut on
pull stroke.

Sliding Dovetail Saw

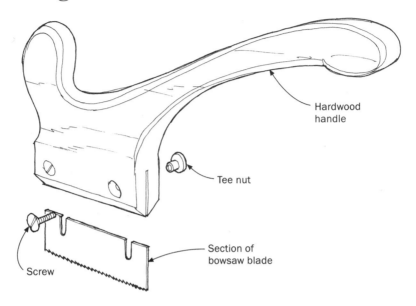

Hardwood
handle

Tee nut

Section of
bowsaw blade

Screw

T O MAKE A SLIDING dovetail saw you will need a piece of hardwood (maple, beech, or fruitwood) 1 in. by 6 in. by 3 in. and
two flat-head ³⁄₁₆- in. by 1-in. bolts with tee-nuts. The blade can be
an old bandsaw or bow sawblade. It should have 10 points to the
inch, although 8 will do. I use a ripsaw blade, which I find cuts better
and faster than a crosscut. The slots allow the blade to be set to the
desired depth.

—Tage Frid, *Middletown, R.I.*

A Better Dovetailing Chisel

ORDINARY CHISELS BOUGHT FOR the purpose of chopping out dovetails are beveled on the top. This bevel, however, is really more of a chamfer that leaves a flat of about $\frac{1}{16}$ in. or so, preventing the chisels from being pushed completely into acute corners. To correct this problem, grind both sides of a square-edged chisel across to a sharp cutting edge. Select an angle slightly less than your usual dovetail angle to allow the tool to trim right into the corner of the tails.

—PERCY W. BLANDFORD, *Stratford-upon-Avon, England*

Grind both sides of chisel
to form sharp edges.

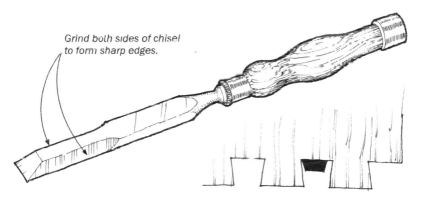

Make edge slope less
than dovetail angle.

Narrow end fits
corners of dovetails.

Wooden Mallet

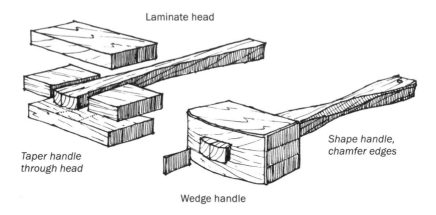

Laminate head

Taper handle
through head

Shape handle,
chamfer edges

Wedge handle

A T LEAST ONE WOODEN carpenter's mallet belongs in every
wood worker's tool chest. The advantages of wood over steel are
obvious—less damage to tools, work, thumbs, and eyes. For the price
of one steel hammer, you can make a dozen mallets, each tailored to a
particular job.

The traditional mallet has a solid-wood head mortised through for
the wedge-shaped handle. My laminated head design is just as strong
and much easier to make. Begin by cutting the handle and two center
laminations for the head from the same 1-in.-thick board (this saves a
lot of fitting later). Copy the handle's wedge angle (no more than ½ in.
of taper) onto one of the side laminations. Then glue up the head
block, carefully aligning the center laminations with the wedge-angle
pencil lines. When the glue has cured, bandsaw the head to shape.
Then chamfer all the edges to reduce the chances of splitting and
insert the handle.

—DANIEL ARNOLD, *Viroqua, Wisc.*

Hammer Shield

I'VE FOUND THAT THE simple hammer shield shown below is great for preventing hammer marks on special projects or woodwork. I made my shield from a small section of discarded steel strapping, which I obtained from a local lumber dealer, but any fairly heavy piece of sheet metal will work equally well. Simply cut a narrow tapered slot in one end for slipping the shield around the nail being driven, and then bend the other end up and out to form a handle. The tapered slot allows the shield to be used for almost any size nail.

—HOWARD E. MOODY, *Upper Jay, N.Y.*

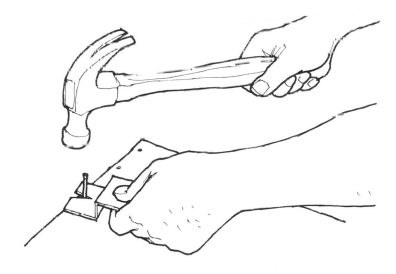

Hammer Hanger

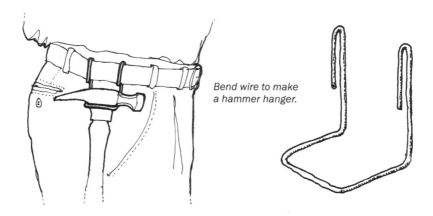

Bend wire to make
a hammer hanger.

FORTY-PLUS YEARS AGO, when I was an apprentice, all tradesmen wore overalls. An old-timer showed me the trick of inserting the hammer's handle into the side opening at the hip below the buttons. Always handy, the hammer's handle hangs along your leg without interfering with movement.

Years later, after the overalls era had passed and leather aprons appeared, I found the hammer loops on the aprons were often in the wrong place for me. So I bent up a piece of ³⁄₁₆-in. wire into a hammer hanger like the one shown above. The hanger slides over your belt to any position you prefer—in my case to the spot where I carried my hammer years ago. Most important, you can drop the hammer in the hanger without looking and retrieve it just as easily.

—JEROME JAHNKE, *Milwaukee, Wisc.*

Plumbing Caps As Tool Ferrules

I USE COMMON HARDWARE-STORE copper plumbing caps for ferrules on my custom turning tools. To use the caps, I turn a tenon on the tool handle to fit the inside diameter of the cap. Then I drill (and file if necessary) an opening in the cap to fit the shank of the tool. After fitting the tool to the handle, I polish the cap and spray it with a clear sealer to keep it looking good. The caps, which average about 40 cents each, are available in sizes from ¼ in. dia. up to 2 in. dia.

—WAYNE KNUTESON, *Murray, Utah*

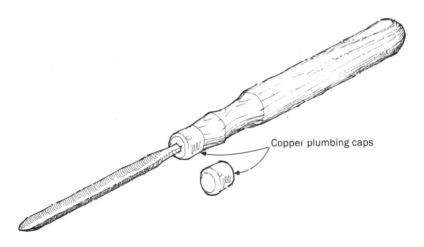

Copper plumbing caps

Guide Blocks for Accurate Hand-Planing

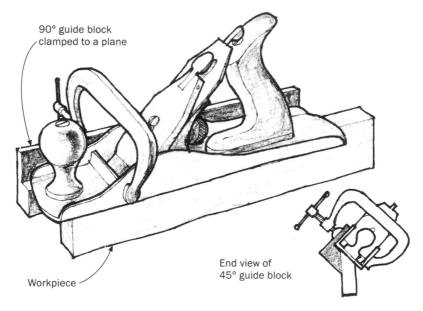

90° guide block clamped to a plane

Workpiece

End view of
45° guide block

BECAUSE I DON'T OWN a jointer, I rely on my bench planes for truing up my lumber. To maintain a consistent angle, I cut guide blocks from scrap pieces of hardwood and clamp them to the plane. I make a few passes, check the angle, then make final adjustments using the plane's lever arm to tilt the blade.

—JACK GABON, *Missoula, Mont.*

Triangular Scraper

THIS GRAUNCHING TOOL (that's what we called it in the old days back in New England) is used for deburring metal, enlarging holes, scraping paint or glue from hard-to-reach places, and many other jobs where a sharp, hard tool is necessary. Break off an old triangular file, hollow-grind it to the shape shown below, and mount in a handle.

—H. NORMAN CAPEN, *Granada Hills, Calif.*

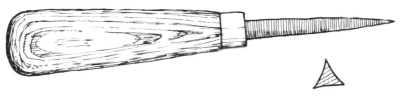

Cross section

Softening Hammer Blows with a Crutch Bottom

FIT AN INEXPENSIVE RUBBER crutch bottom on your hammer to knock apart antiques or assemble new cabinets without damage.

—ADAM LEMPEL, *Chesterfield, N.H.*

Cleaning File Teeth

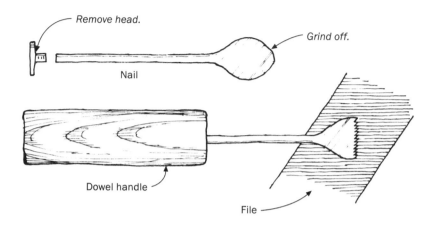

A BLIND SHARPENING-SHOP OPERATOR showed me this simple file-cleaning tool—it works better than a file brush. Hammer flat the pointed end of a 16d or 20d nail and grind the front edge straight. Remove the head of the nail and fit into a drilled dowel handle. Now push the straight edge of the tool along the grooves of file teeth. Soon tiny teeth will form in the edge of the tool that push metal, grease, and rust out of the file. Turn the tool on edge to remove stubborn particles in one or two file grooves.

—JOHN FOOTE, *Clarksville, Tenn.*

Covering Sharp Tool Tips
with Wine Bottle Corks

USE WINE BOTTLE CORKS to cover the tips of scratch awls, compass points, and the like. The corks keep the points of your tools sharp, and they also protect your fingers when you're rummaging through the toolbox.

—TONY KONOVALOFF, *Tahoe Paradise, Calif.*

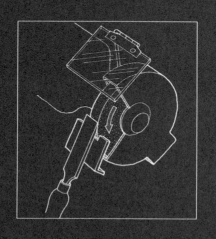

[*Chapter 4*]

SHARPENING & GRINDING

Sharpening a Chisel with Abrasive Paper

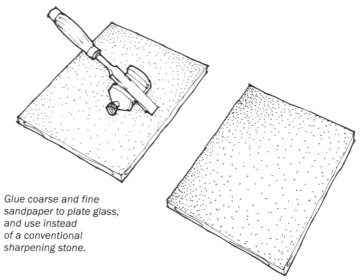

Glue coarse and fine
sandpaper to plate glass,
and use instead
of a conventional
sharpening stone.

H ERE'S A QUICK WAY to produce a really sharp edge on a chisel or
plane iron without the typical problems of holding the tool by
hand on a grinder, such as overheating an edge or dealing with
unevenly worn sharpening stones. Attach full sheets of 150-grit and
600-grit wet-or-dry abrasive paper to ¼-in.-thick plate glass with spray
adhesive. Place your chisel in a wheeled sharpening guide, and begin
with the 150 grit. Spray a little water for lubricant, and go to work.
You will quickly produce a flat bevel, even on the widest chisel. Now
go to the 600 grit, again with water. The sharpening guide ensures
that you will get exactly the same angle on the subsequent, finer honing, and in no time you'll have a sharpened edge that almost looks
polished. If you want to polish further, finer paper up to 2000 grit is
available.

This method also works for truing the bottom of a plane or the flat
side of a chisel.

—THOMAS R. SCHRUNK, *Minneapolis, Minn.*

Sharpening Guide for a Grinding Wheel

I REMOVED THE GUIDES (tool rests) that came with my grinder and replaced them with a single piece of steel angle that spans both wheels. I use this guide for normal grinding. Then I made a sliding wooden carriage that correctly angles chisels and plane irons. This arrangement lets me switch quickly between straight and angled grinding. I use 80-grit, white aluminum-oxide wheels, which run cooler than standard wheels.

—FRANK NORMAN, *South Perth, Western Australia*

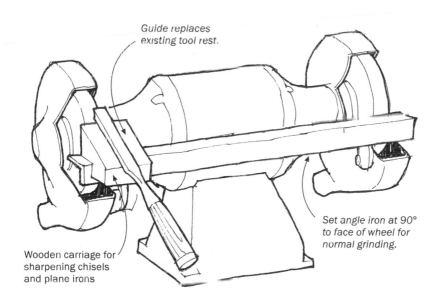

Guide replaces existing tool rest.

Set angle iron at 90° to face of wheel for normal grinding.

Wooden carriage for sharpening chisels and plane irons

Constant-Angle Honing

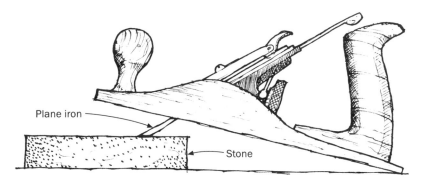

Plane iron

Stone

M OST OF US KNOW an old-timer who has demonstrated a method of work so effective and simple you wonder why it never occurred to you before. This happened to me recently while honing my plane iron. I was struggling to maintain a constant angle against the stone, lamenting that I did not have one of those fancy roller tools that locks the plane iron at a constant angle while rolling it across the abrasive. Here's a simple solution:

Slide the chip breaker back from the cutting edge about ¾ in. Then lock the double iron in the plane with the blade extending through the throat about ½ in. With the heel on the bench top and the plane iron on the stone, slide the plane back and forth. The setup holds the iron at a constant angle to the stone to grind a perfect secondary bevel.

You may have to adjust the setup slightly to fit different-size plane bodies, stones, and bevel angles, but the basic idea seems to work with any plane.

—JAMES VASI, *Cheektowaga, N.Y.*

Plane-Iron Honing Tool

H ERE'S A SIMPLE, INEXPENSIVE jig for honing slotted plane irons
Just attach a 4-in.-long, ¾-in. or ⁵⁄₁₆-in. carriage bolt to the iron,
as shown in the sketch below. The round head of the bolt slides easily
on the bench, maintaining a constant honing angle. For fine adjustment or for honing microbevels, you can shim the stone, or twist the
bolt up or down a hair.

—PAUL WEISSMAN, *Centerville, Ohio*

Nail Polish Shows Honing Progress

A PPLY A THIN COAT of nail polish to the cutting edge of chisels
and plane irons before sharpening. The wear pattern in the color
will give you direct feedback about the sharpening angle and honing
progress.

—HOWARD E. MOODY, *Upper Jay, N.Y.*

Regrinding Plane Irons

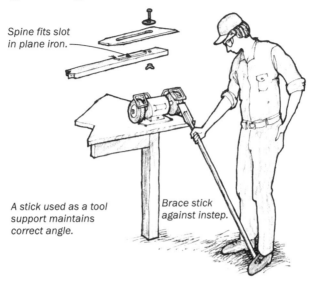

Spine fits slot in plane iron.

A stick used as a tool support maintains correct angle.

Brace stick against instep.

W ITH A SIMPLE STICK JIG you can quickly, easily and accurately regrind plane irons on a bench grinder, and it's more fun than you can imagine. Select a good, stiff hardwood stick—mine is 44 in. long. Add a short wooden spine (to fit the iron's screw slot) and a stove-bolt/washer arrangement to hold the iron in place. Now, keeping the stick in line with the wheel, brace the stick against the inside of your left foot and lightly arc the iron across the wheel. The stick can be picked up to check the progress of the grind, then—as long as you don't move your foot—returned to the same spot against your shoe.

The resulting blade grind won't be perfectly straight but crowned ever so slightly. This convex profile will prove superior to a straight profile for most hand-planing applications and is tricky to achieve any other way.

—PAUL D. FRANK, *Fond du Lac, Wisc.*

Hazardless Honing

HERE IS A SIMPLE COMBINATION storage box and jig that will enable you to use your oilstones more effectively and safely. What makes the box unique is a wide tongue cut into the bottom. In use, the tongue is secured in a woodworking vise, ensuring a stable, firm foundation for the oilstone.

To make the box, cut blocks for the base and cover from any hardwood. Use a drill press with a multispur or Forstner bit to remove most of the waste. The cavity in the base should be about half as deep as the stone. The cavity in the cover should be $\frac{1}{16}$ in. or so deeper to provide clearance. Chop out the remaining waste with a chisel, making sure the stone fits snug in the base and doesn't rock. To complete the box, saw away the bottom corners of the base to leave the tongue

—AL CHING, *Fullerton, Calif.*

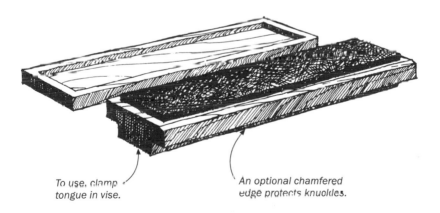

To use, clamp tongue in vise.

An optional chamfered edge protects knuckles.

Sharpening a Scraper

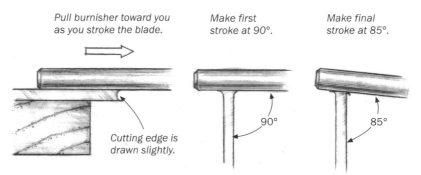

Pull burnisher toward you as you stroke the blade.

Make first stroke at 90°.

Make final stroke at 85°.

Cutting edge is drawn slightly.

90°

85°

TURNING A GOOD EDGE on a hand or cabinet scraper is a recurring problem among many woodworkers. Here are some tips.

After the scraper edge is polished and square to the smooth sides (no file marks), many workers frequently neglect to burnish the broad, flat surface of the scraper. This step must be done carefully if you want to obtain a good hook on the cutting edge.

With the scraper lying flat, close to the workbench edge, burnish each flat side, keeping the burnisher flat on the side of the scraper. I draw the cutting edge slightly by pulling the burnisher toward me with long, firm strokes. Under magnification you would actually see two ears protruding above the scraper sides, as shown in the above drawing.

In preparation for burnishing the top edge of the blade, first put a drop or two of oil on the burnisher. Place the burnisher flat on the far end of the scraper, held vertically in a vise, and firmly pull it toward you. Two or three strokes should do; the first at 90° and then with the handle lowered slightly at 85° to the side of the scraper, as shown in the drawing. It is important to hold the burnisher firmly by the handle and make long, slicing strokes, which extend over a large section of the blade. This will keep the blade smooth and prevent nicks or grooves in the edge.

As you may know, scraper blades come in different thicknesses. In your initial efforts, you may find thin blades easier to sharpen. As you become more adept, you may prefer thicker blades, which hold an edge longer.

—KELLY MEHLER, Berea, Ky.,
from a question by Glenn Marchione, Penndel, Pa.

Recipe for Razor-Sharp Carving Tools

DURING MY 50 YEARS OF carving I have collected some 280 edge tools, which, for the kind of carving I do, must be kept sharp enough to shave with. To prepare the edge, I use three grades of progressively finer India stones. But the real trick is to strop the edge to a mirror finish. For this you'll need a couple of pieces of sole leather from your local shoe shop and an abrasive product called Cloverleaf Abrasive Compound, which was originally manufactured for grinding engine valves on Model T Fords. It is a smooth-cutting abrasive suspended in a Vaseline-like jelly. Cloverleaf is still manufactured today in seven different abrasive grades and can be bought in most auto supply stores. You will need two grades—I use one up from finest and two down from coarsest.

First, soak the pieces of sole leather in light lubricating oil. Then rub about a teaspoon of the finer abrasive into the smooth side of one piece and a like amount of the coarser abrasive into the rough side of the other piece. Bend the leather into the profile of the cutting edge and strop both the inside and outside of the carving gouge to produce an incredibly sharp edge.

—FORD GREEN, San Antonio, Tex.

Sharpening a Woodcarving V-Gouge

T O SHARPEN A V-GOUGE, first square off the cutting edge by holding the tool vertically and working the edge against the sharpening stone. This will angle the edge 90° to the shaft of the tool. Next, treat each side of the V as if it were a flat chisel and sharpen each outside bevel to a 15° angle. Be careful that both bevels are the same and don't round off the corners. A sharp hook will usually form at the point where the two sides of the V meet. Remove this by sharpening the point as if it were a miniature gouge—rock the tool back and forth across the stone, angling this lower bevel about 25°. In time, the hook and any excess will wear away and you will have an even, sharp edge.

Next, strop the tool on a piece of leather or a cloth buffing wheel until all of the wire burrs are removed. The tool bevels, both inside and out, should be polished to a mirror shine. You can hone the inside bevels with a fine Arkansas slip, but avoid trying to sharpen the inside of the V to a perfectly acute angle. Instead, the inner angle should be treated as a small radius, and should blend into the flat planes on either side. Sharpened in this manner, your gouge will cut more efficiently and will be easier to control around curves.

RICK BUTZ, *Blue Mountain Lake, N.Y.*,
from a question by B. W. Thompson, Dobbs Ferry, N.Y.

Flattening Oilstones

TO FLATTEN AN OILSTONE, take a flat piece of plate glass or steel, sprinkle about ¼ cup of 80-grit carborundum powder (available from any lapidary supply house) onto the center of the glass, and pour about ¼ cup of water into the grit. Grind the stone in a circular motion, using as much of the glass surface as possible. Keep heavy pressure on the stone as you grind. I always flatten the coarsest stone first, while the grit is cutting fastest, then move on to the fine stones as the grit wears. Check the stone with a straightedge after washing the grit off and drying the stone with paper towels. After flattening about a dozen stones, the glass itself will probably become slightly hollow and must be replaced.

Waterstones are even easier to flatten. Some workers flatten them by rubbing two waterstones together. You can also put a piece of 220-grit wet/dry sandpaper on a piece of plate glass, flood the paper with water and grind the stone with a circular motion on the paper. If you have both waterstones and oilstones, use different pieces of glass to avoid contaminating the waterstones with oil. Wash the stone and paper frequently by dipping them in a bucket of water, and dry the stone with paper towels before checking with a straightedge.

The type of stone you use is a matter of preference. For years I recommended a medium India, then a fine Arkansas oilstone as the best method to get a good best edge. I now think the edges possible with waterstones are even better.

—IAN KIRBY, *Cumming, Ga.,*
from a question by Mark Pratt, Nickliff, Ohio

Grit-Slurry Sharpening

TO ADD EVEN MORE lore to a subject many craftsmen approach with mystic reverence, here's yet another sharpening method. The method uses a slurry of loose grit on a flat glass plate and is effective for sharpening woodworking tools, particularly plane irons. It is the same method laboratories use to sharpen the microtome, an instrument that slices tissue into thin sections for microscopic examination.

Start by dumping ½ teaspoon of 400 grit on an 8-in. by 8-in. pane of glass, adding several drops of light machine oil to make a slurry. Hone the plane iron as though you were using a bench stone. When you obtain a good bevel, wipe the glass clean and repeat the process using 600 grit to obtain the final cutting edge. For optimum results, polish with a polishing compound or give the blade a few strokes on a leather strop.

This method is superior in several ways to sharpening on a stone. The glass is flat and wears little, even with much use, and the large surface area allows for a more comfortable hand motion. The large surface is particularly suitable for the use of a roller device to hone the iron at a constant angle. Finally, you can buy a wide range of abrasive powders at hobby shops that deal in lapidary supplies (one source is Grieger's Inc., 900 S. Arroyo Parkway, Pasadena, CA 91109). A small investment in materials will allow you to perform work that would otherwise require several different grades of stones.

—GEORGE MUSTOE, *Bellingham, Wash.*

Stone Hook

FOR YEARS, I HAVE COLLECTED sharpening stones from yard sales and happily used them in my workshop. Because no two stones are the same size, I built a simple device that I can adapt to hold stones of different length and width. I call it a stone hook, and the design is based on that of a bench hook. The device is a simple wooden block fitted with a fence at each end. A pair of wedges lock the stones into the block against a spacer piece sized for each stone. Wedge the stone into the block, and then clamp the block onto the workbench with the bench vise.

– JAMES SCALONE, *San Diego, Calif.*

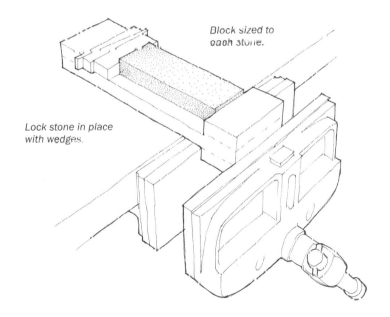

Block sized to each stone.

Lock stone in place with wedges.

Care of Japanese Sharpening Stones

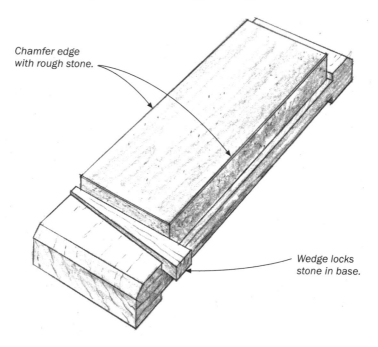

Chamfer edge with rough stone.

Wedge locks stone in base.

T HERE ARE TWO TYPES of Japanese waterstones, synthetic and natural. Synthetic waterstones may be placed in water to soak for 10 to 20 minutes before use, which is what I do, or kept in water all the time. Keep natural stones dry except when in use and protect them from freezing. I always make a wooden base for my stones, as shown in the drawing above.

Compared with oilstones, Japanese waterstones are quite soft, so they wear more quickly. A flat stone is essential for a sharp blade, so sharpen across the stone from corner to corner as evenly as possible and frequently turn the stone end for end so that it wears evenly. Narrow chisels will wear a hollow in the middle of a stone, so don't sharpen a wide blade on a stone that's been used for narrow blades.

I recommend two separate sets of stones: one for narrow blades and one for wide blades like plane blades. (A good beginning set of manmade stones is 800X, 1200X, and 6000X or 8000X.) If you have only one set of stones, use different surfaces for chisels and plane blades.

Waterstones are easy to reflatten. First, get a sheet of glass about 16-in. square and at least ¼ in. thick. Round the corners and chamfer the edges of the glass with silicon-carbide sandpaper. Place a wet sheet of wet/dry silicon-carbide paper on the glass—it will stick by suction. Use 80- or 100-grit paper if your stone is in poor condition, 150- or 180-grit paper for a slightly hollowed stone, and 320- to 600-grit paper for slightly hollowed 6000X or 8000X manmade finishing stones or natural finishing stones. While splashing on water, rub the stone on the sandpaper in a circular motion until the entire surface touches the paper. This is all you need to do for most stones.

For a perfect surface on a natural finishing stone or a 6000X or 8000X manmade finishing stone, after flattening, rub two finishing stones together with plenty of water until the faces fit tightly and are difficult to move. Don't rub a natural stone against a manmade stone. Stones that are badly worn can be rubbed on a concrete surface or on a concrete block with plenty of water before going to the paper. After flattening a stone, chamfer all the edges with a rough stone to avoid chipping.

—TOSHIO ODATE, *Woodbury, Conn.,*
from a question by D. Christenson, Solebury, Pa.

Lineshaft Sharpening

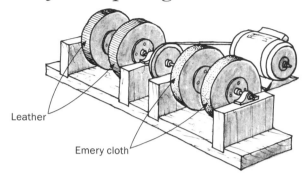

Leather

Emery cloth

THIS INEXPENSIVE SHARPENING SETUP puts a keen edge on tools in seconds without the usual heat buildup problems of powered abrasive wheels. To construct the setup, laminate four 7-in. wheel blanks from plywood or particleboard. Epoxy the blanks to shaft collars, which are set-screwed to the ½-in. lineshaft. The shaft turns in pillow blocks mounted on an oak frame. If a lathe is not available, the wheel blanks can be trued right on the lineshaft with a chisel and a temporary tool rest.

Cement emery-cloth strips (80 grit and 320 grit) to two of the wheels, lining the wheels first with burlap-backed cork (available from a linoleum dealer). Cement leather to the other two wheels. Mount the leather flesh side out to one wheel and hair side out to the other. Charge the "flesh" wheel with emery, the "hair" wheel with rouge. Using rubber cement for all mountings will make replacement easier later on.

An old ¼-hp appliance motor will provide sufficient power. Size the motor and lineshaft pulleys so the wheels turn at 500 to 600 rpm up and away from the operator.

Dull tools may need treatment on all four wheels, but most tools can be sharpened on only the finer two or three wheels.

—ROBERT L. KOCH, *Tarlsio, Mo.*

[84]

Sharpening Jig
for a Stationary Belt Sander

TO SHARPEN CHISELS and other tools, I screwed a small 30° block of wood to the back side of the stop bar on my stationary belt sander. I use a 220-grit belt and make sure the back of the tool is flat against the block when I press the blade against the moving belt. The longer belt on the stationary machine helps prevent overheating and softening the edge of the tool.

Because I grind most of my tools at 30°, I usually leave the block at that setting (it does not interfere with the normal use of the sander). But if I need a different setting, I can loosen the stop-bar attachment and pivot the block to any angle between 25° and 40°. One thing to remember. If you have a dust collector connected to your sander, disconnect it when sharpening tools. The sparks could start a fire.

—BOB KELLAND, *St. John's, Newfoundland*

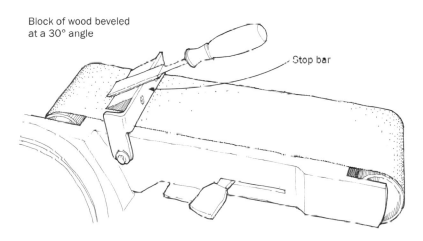

Block of wood beveled
at a 30° angle

Stop bar

Stationary belt sander

Which Way Should a Bench Grinder Rotate?

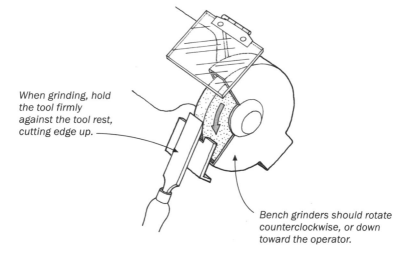

When grinding, hold the tool firmly against the tool rest, cutting edge up.

Bench grinders should rotate counterclockwise, or down toward the operator.

M ANY WOODWORKERS ARE CONFUSED about the proper rotation of a bench grinder, whether it should rotate toward the operator or away. The majority of commercial grinders are designed to rotate toward the operator while a tool rest supports the chisel or plane iron at a fixed angle (see the drawing above). Maintaining a proper grinding angle is crucial to sharpening success. With the wheel turning down toward you and into the tool and the tool held firmly on the tool rest, you can obtain a consistent hollow bevel across the end of the tool.

If you reversed your grinder so that it rotated away from you, the wheel (trying to carry the tool around in this rotation) would tend to lift the tool off the tool rest. This would make it difficult for you to do accurate work and could be dangerous if the chisel or plane iron got away from you.

Another way to think about it is to realize your grinder is a cutting tool, like your jointer or table saw. Generally, the workpiece is fed into the tool, against the rotation of the cutter, blade, or grinding wheel. With the proper guards (or tool rest, in this case) and technique, the work can be done accurately and safely.

One note of extreme caution: A buffing wheel mounted on a grinder presents a serious danger if improperly used. Tools being buffed are held with their cutting edge down (see the drawing below). Cloth buffing wheels are much softer than grinding wheels. It's easy to catch a tool edge in a buffing wheel if the tool edge is presented in the same way it is to the grinding wheel. Catching the edge of a cutting tool in a buffing wheel almost inevitably results in the tool being thrown violently onto the floor (or into your foot). If you use a buffing wheel on a bench grinder, it is imperative that you point your tool down, so the buffing wheel can't catch the edge.

—GARY ROGOWSKI, *Portland, Ore.,*
from a question by Craig Masciolo, Paradise Valley, Ariz.

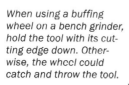

When using a buffing wheel on a bench grinder, hold the tool with its cutting edge down. Otherwise, the wheel could catch and throw the tool.

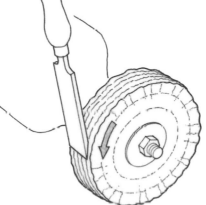

Lubricating Sharpening Stones with Kerosene

KEROSENE IS A GREAT LUBRICANT for sharpening stones. It is inexpensive, commonly available, and has a slightly oily quality that lubricates well. I use it on my water, oil, ceramic, and diamond stones. In addition, kerosene is a great brush-cleaning solvent, safer than gasoline and cheaper than mineral spirits.

—ROBERT E. STEELE, *Allegan, Mich.*

Sharpening with Abrasive Compounds

IN MY SHOP, I'VE replaced the sharpening stone and strop with a two-wheel buffer and two abrasive compounds commonly used by knifemakers and gunsmiths. First, I grind the tool's edge on a regular grinding wheel, then I buff the edge on a muslin buffing wheel loaded with a greaseless buffing compound manufactured by Lea Manufacturing Co. (available from Badger Shooter's Supply, Box 397, Owen, WI 54460; 715-229-2101). Even its fine grade cuts fast enough to send a few sparks flying, so I quench the tool often to prevent heat build-up. Next, I polish the edge with white No. 555 Polish-O-Ray (available from Brownells Inc., Route 2, Box 1, Montezuma, IA 50171; 515-623-5401). Alternate polishing the top and bottom of the cutting edge. Only a light touch is required to finish the edge to perfection.

—ROBERT MORDINI, *Edmond, Okla.*

Hardening Tools That Won't Stay Sharp

I F YOU HAVE DESTROYED the hardness in your carbon-steel edge tools by overheating (turning the edge blue while regrinding), here's how to reharden the cutting edge with a relatively simple, three-step process:

1. Annealing. Heat each tool slowly and thoroughly to about 1,450°F (a bright cherry red); a propane torch works fine. Then bury it in a large container of sand, allowing the tool to cool slowly. If the tool's edge can be readily filed when it has cooled, then it has been properly annealed.

2. Hardening. After restoring the cutting edge to its original shape, reheat the tool to 1,450°F, and then quench it by plunging the tool edge first into a container of soft water. Agitate until it's cool. Run a new smooth file over the edge. If the file skates over the edge without catching, the tool has been properly hardened. It is now too hard to use, though, so it must be tempered first.

3. Tempering. Heating and quenching the tool blackens the tip, so polish it with a piece of fine-grit wet-or-dry sandpaper as soon as you've checked for hardness with the file. Heat the tool slowly with a propane torch, keeping the flame well back of the edge. When the edge turns a soft yellow, quench again in soft water.

Heat-treating carving tools in this manner takes practice, so don't be discouraged if you have some failures. But learning the art of heat treating can pay big dividends.

For more detailed information, find a used copy of *Hardening and Tempering Engineer's Tools* by George Gentry, Argus Books Ltd. (the book is out of print). It's a good, basic book on the subject.

—RAY LARSEN, *Hanover, Mass.,*
from a question by Steve Hamrell, Park City, Mont.

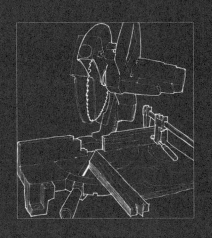

Chapter 5

PORTABLE POWER-TOOL FIXTURES

Chopsaw Stop Block

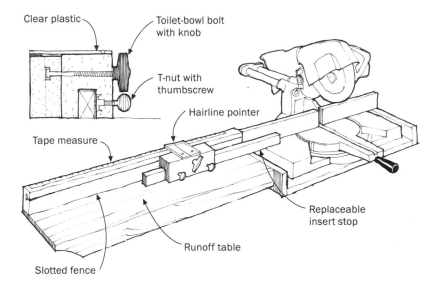

Clear plastic
Toilet-bowl bolt with knob
T-nut with thumbscrew
Hairline pointer
Tape measure
Replaceable insert stop
Runoff table
Slotted fence

T HIS CHOPSAW STOP BLOCK has worked wonderfully for me. It speeds up my crosscut work significantly, and I never use a tape measure at the saw anymore. A special feature of the stop block is the replaceable insert, which ensures perfect-length cuts. To align the stop, set the hairline pointer (marked on a piece of clear plastic) to zero, slide the insert past the sawblade, tighten everything up, and cut off the insert, which zeroes it. Now you can slide the pointer to whatever measurement you need, tighten the stop-block knob, and cut with confidence.

—LARS MIKKELSEN, *Santa Margarita, Calif.*

Cutting Angles Greater Than 45° on a Chopsaw

FOR A RECENT PROJECT, I needed to make 50° miter cuts, but my power miter saw cut only up to 47°. To remedy that problem, I made a fixture that clamps to the main fence with the working edge 90° to the saw's original fence.

Now, to cut large angles, all I have to do is set the saw at the reciprocal of the angle (90° minus 50° gives a saw setting of 40°). When you cut angles more than 60°, it is a good idea to use a workpiece hold-down to keep your fingers away from the blade.

—RICHARD A. MENIN, *Meadowbrook, Pa.*

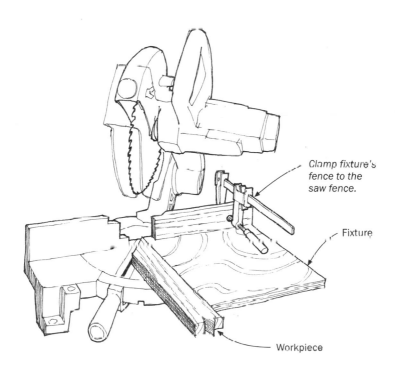

Clamp fixture's fence to the saw fence.

Fixture

Workpiece

Production Setup for the Chopsaw

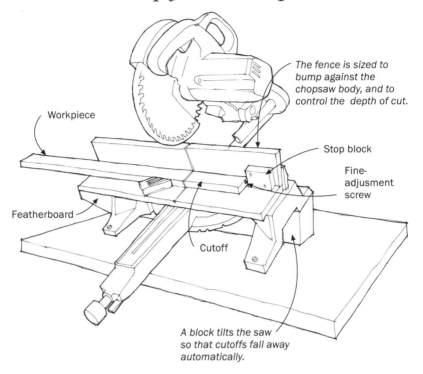

The fence is sized to bump against the chopsaw body, and to control the depth of cut.

Workpiece

Stop block

Fine-adjusment screw

Featherboard

Cutoff

A block tilts the saw so that cutoffs fall away automatically.

W HEN CUTTING HUNDREDS OF identical pieces of wood to length for production work, a chopsaw is essential but not sufficient. To speed up cutting time, you need automatic removal of the sawn pieces. The easiest way to achieve this is to tilt the saw forward by attaching a 5-in. spacer board underneath the rear of the saw.

A simple jig is then clamped to the saw table to give you accurate results. The floor of the jig should be melamine or vinyl-coated to allow the pieces to slide off the jig easily. Secure the jig firmly to the saw. To help avoid tearout, screw a fence to the back edge of the jig. Cut the fence to the proper height so that it bumps against the saw body and acts as a depth stop, too.

On the fence at the distance of the cut plus ½ in., screw a stop block equipped with a flat-head screw for fine adjustment and sawdust clearance. Finally, you need to screw a featherboard to the floor of the jig to keep the workpiece against the fence.

This jig is so easy to build that you can have one for each length you need to cut. The time spent building the jig will be saved the very first time you use it.

—KLAS WILZEN, *Glimmingeg, Malmo, Sweden*

Measuring a Stop Block for a Power Miter Box

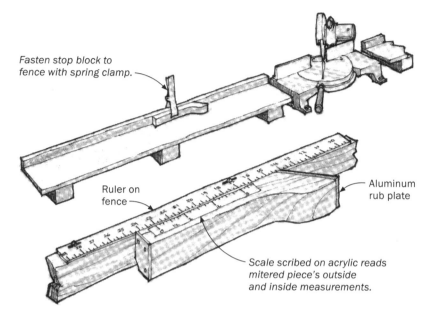

Fasten stop block to fence with spring clamp.

Ruler on fence

Aluminum rub plate

Scale scribed on acrylic reads mitered piece's outside and inside measurements.

I F YOU CUT LOTS OF 45° miters on a power miter box, this device will save you hours of measuring. The scale on the stop block lets you set up quickly for either inside or outside measurements on a mitered frame.

To make the stop block, carefully miter a hardwood 1x2 and band-saw to the shape shown. For a touch of class, install a ⅛-in.-thick aluminum rub plate to the face of the block. Screw a 6-in. length of acrylic to the top of the block and carefully scribe a measurement scale into the plastic. The measurement scale should be laid out in inches, but the numbering halved so that 1 in. is marked ½ and 2 in. is marked 1, etc. This scale will be used to set inside measurements as explained on the facing page.

If your saw doesn't have an inch scale along the fence, mount a metal yardstick to the top of the fence. Use slotted holes so you can fine-tune the position of the scale to reflect exact measurements.

To use the stop block for outside measurement miter cuts, simply align the zero mark on the stop block with the appropriate outside measure on the fence scale. To use the block for inside measurements, first measure the width of your molding. Find the mark on the stop block that corresponds to the width and align that mark with the inside measure on the fence scale. For example, if your molding is 2 in. wide and the desired inside measure is 19 in., then find 2 on the stop block and align it with 19 on the fence side.

For added convenience, construct the stop block with a square end so it can be flipped and used for cutting pieces with square ends. Scribe a mark on another side of the stop block to align the square end with the fence scale. In use, fasten the stop block to the fence with a spring clamp or a small C-clamp.

—DEAN FRENCH, *Kapaa, Kauai, Hawaii*

Cutting Sheet Goods with a Circular Saw

Trim plywood to width with a circular saw.

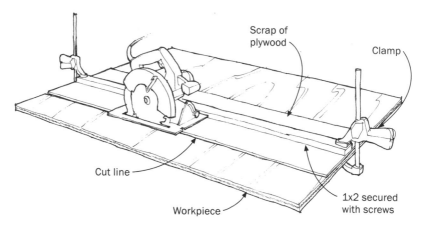

Scrap of plywood

Clamp

Cut line

Workpiece

1x2 secured with screws

THIS FIXTURE FOR CUTTING sheet goods with a circular saw is simple to make and gives accurate results. Attach a 4-ft. or 8-ft. length of 1x2 lumber to the middle of a piece of plywood that is the same length and about 12 in. wide. With the saw's base bearing against the 1x2, which is the fence of the fixture, rip off the edges of the plywood. You're done. Attach this jig to anything at any angle, putting the edge of the jig right on the cut line. You will know exactly where your saw will cut. Splintering is eliminated underneath the guide. Rip one edge at 45° if you like—it could come in handy.

The accuracy of this fixture depends on a straight fence, so pay attention when you attach the 1x2. Use a 4-ft. or 8-ft. straightedge, or just use the factory edge of a piece of plywood.

—GARY ALLAN MAY, *Seattle, Wash.*

Circular-Saw Cutting Template

I OFTEN CUT SHEETS OF plywood with my circular saw, but it can be difficult to place a fence the correct distance from the cut line to guide the saw. To solve this problem, I made the template shown below. It's much easier to position a fence using the template than using the saw base.

To make the template, I clamped a ⅛-in. piece of hardboard to my saw's baseplate. Then I trimmed the hardboard to the exact size of the plate with a router and a flush-trimming bit. Using a saw, I nipped cuts in the front and rear of the template to show the location of the blade.

Now when I want to cut plywood, I just draw a pencil line where I want the cut and then align the fence (I use a Clamp 'N Tool Guide, made by Griset Industries; 800-662-2892). It's quick and easy to place the fence on either side of the cut with the kerf on the waste side of the line.

—Rasjad Lints, *Vancouver, Wa.*

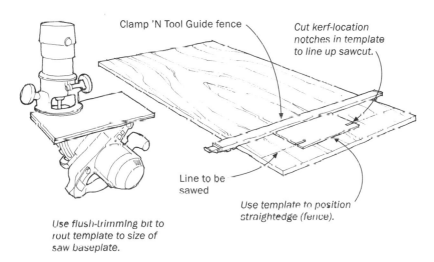

Clamp 'N Tool Guide fence

Cut kerf-location notches in template to line up sawcut.

Line to be sawed

Use template to position straightedge (fence).

Use flush-trimming bit to rout template to size of saw baseplate.

"Poor-Boy" Radial-Arm Saw

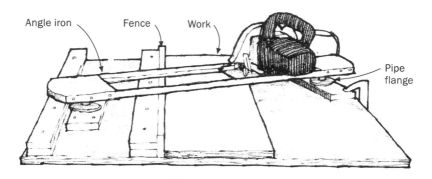

Angle iron — Fence — Work — Pipe flange

FOR CROSSCUTTING LONG BOARDS and making miter cuts, this shopmade saw guide is accurate, portable, easy to use and economical to build.

The guide is simply an angle-iron and plywood track sized to fit the base of a portable circular saw. The guide is perched atop legs at each end. Each leg is made from a pair of 3½-in. pipe flanges connected by a ¾-in. by 1½-in. pipe nipple. The legs provide clearance for the work and allow the track to pivot for making angle cuts.

To use, clamp the guide at the proper angle in relation to the fence on the plywood base. Before cutting, secure the saw's blade guard up out of the way with a screw threaded through a hole in the blade housing. Make sure you remove the screw before the saw is used in the conventional manner.

Another note of caution: The direction of blade rotation tends to lift the work from the table, so make sure the work is tight against the fence and can't shift. Otherwise, the work might pinch the sawblade and cause the saw to lift out of the guide rails.

On my 7¼-in. saw, the depth of cut is limited to 1¼ in., but this covers most of the crosscutting work I do.

—JACK FISHER, *Dayton, Ohio*

Cutoff Table

B ACK IN THE DAYS before I had a radial-arm saw in my shop, I worked out a cutoff table to use with my portable circular saw. The fixture consists of a 2x12 table, a 2x4 fence, and a guide bridge. The rabbets on the two bridge pieces should face each other and be spaced just wide enough to fit the base of your portable circular saw. If desired, a stop block can be C-clamped to the fence for accurate duplicate cutoff work.

—C. G. FADER, *Ketchikan, Alaska*

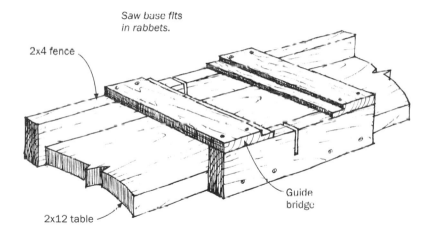

Saw base fits
in rabbets.

2x4 fence

Guide
bridge

2x12 table

Shop-Built Panel Saw

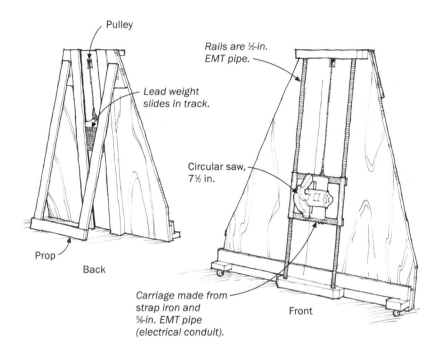

Pulley

Rails are ½-in.
EMT pipe.

Lead weight
slides in track.

Circular saw,
7½ in.

Prop

Back

Carriage made from
strap iron and
⅜-in. EMT pipe
(electrical conduit).

Front

AFTER WRESTLING 4x8 PLYWOOD panels around my shop for 45 years, I finally decided to build a panel saw. The design I used is simple and inexpensive; the fixture's components and construction details are shown in the sketch above. The only tricky part is the carriage.

For the carriage sliders, split two pieces of ⅜-in. EMT pipe (electrical conduit) end to end. Spread the cut, or squeeze until the sliders have a nice sliding fit on the ½-in. rails. Bend the ends of the crosspieces up to conform to the radius of the tubing. With the sliders and crosspieces clamped in place on the rails, tack-weld the pieces together. Check the carriage to make sure it is square and slides smoothly. If all is well, remove the carriage, and braze all four corners. Now position your saw on the carriage, drill mounting holes, and fasten the saw to the carriage. To keep the carriage running smoothly, keep a little paraffin or light grease on the rails.

I made the saw counterbalance weight by melting down some lead and pouring it into a rectangular mold. The counterbalance should be slightly heavier than the saw so that the saw will stay parked at the top of the rails.

—WILLIAM SKINNER, *Everett, Wash.*

Homemade Bit for Deep Holes

TO DRILL HOLES FOR LONG threaded rods, I hammered one end of a 26-in. steel rod flat and sharpened it as shown in the sketch below. The bit won't pull chips out of the hole like an expensive ship's auger, so you'll have to retract it more often to clear the chips. Considering the savings, this is a minor inconvenience.

—RALPH ZWIESLER, *Freesoil, Mich.*

Hammer end of rod flat and sharpen.

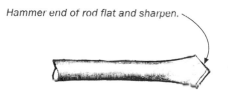

Biscuit-Joined Edge-Banding

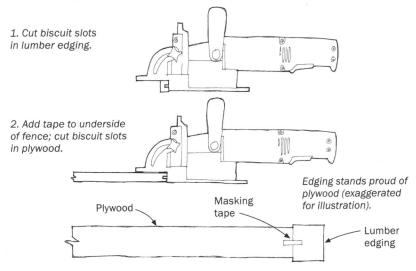

1. Cut biscuit slots
in lumber edging.

2. Add tape to underside
of fence; cut biscuit slots
in plywood.

Edging stands proud of
plywood (exaggerated
for illustration).

Plywood

Masking
tape

Lumber
edging

B ISCUIT JOINTS ARE AN effective way to attach solid-wood edging
to plywood or medium-density fiberboard (MDF). But I like to
offset the biscuit slots a bit to ensure that the edge-banding is slightly
raised above the surface of the plywood. Otherwise, the edging will
sometimes dip slightly below the surface of the veneer.

You may be tempted to offset the slot by adjusting the fence, but
don't do it. It's not only time-consuming but risky, because the fence
can sometimes end up slightly out of parallel to the first slot. Cut the
slots in the edging first, and then add one or two layers of masking
tape at the front and back of the fence before you cut the slots in
the plywood.

The masking tape will slightly offset the slots by just the right
amount. A skewed block or smoothing plane will trim the edging
flush to the veneered plywood.

—KEN SHAW, San Diego, Calif.

Screw-Pocket Drilling Jig

T HIS JIG MAKES IT SIMPLE to drill screw pockets for securing a tabletop to its apron. Start with a 1-in.-sq. by 4-in.-long hardwood block, and drill a ⅜-in. hole in the end of the block as deep as your drill will reach. Draw the profile of the hole on the side of the block, and decide how deep and at what angle (usually 25° or so) you want your pocket. Then draw a line across the block to define the pocket, and saw the pieces in two along this angled line. Glue the sawn-off waste onto the other side of the block, as shown, to re-create a square corner. Now clamp the block to a scrap piece, and test-drill a pocket. Trim the end of the block to make the pocket deeper, if necessary. After you've drilled the pockets in the apron, finish by drilling screw-shank holes through the pockets with a hand-held drill.

—E. G. LINCOLN, *Parsippany, N.J.*

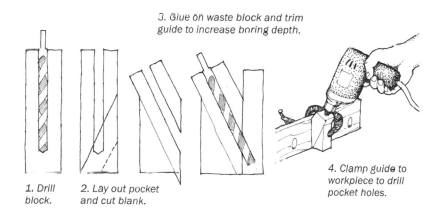

3. Glue on waste block and trim guide to increase boring depth.

1. Drill block.

2. Lay out pocket and cut blank.

4. Clamp guide to workpiece to drill pocket holes.

Horizontal Boring Jig

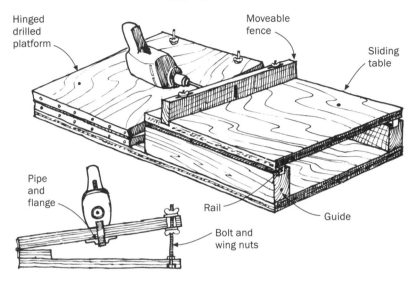

Hinged drilled platform

Moveable fence

Sliding table

Pipe and flange

Rail

Guide

Bolt and wing nuts

M Y BORING JIG, WHICH uses a ½-in. portable drill, is similar to a conventional horizontal-boring machine except that the table moves rather than the drill. The jig consists of a base, a hinged drill platform, and a sliding table.

Make the base and sliding table from ¾-in. hardwood plywood. The drill platform should be extra stiff, so laminate two pieces of ½-in. plywood to give a 1-in.-thick platform. Spindle elevation is adjusted by raising or lowering the hinged drill platform. Install a piano hinge on one edge and two or three bolts with wing nuts for adjustment on the other edge. If adjustment is needed over a wide range (say, 3 in.), some sort of pivoting arrangement would be required for the adjustment bolts.

Most ½-in. drills have a threaded handle socket on the top or side that accept standard ¾-in. threaded pipe. Secure the drill to the platform with a short piece of threaded pipe and a standard floor flange.

Elevating the platform swings the drill through a short arc, so the fence on the sliding table must be mounted through slotted bolt holes to allow for movement. Hardwood rails on the bottom of the table mated with hardwood guide blocks on the base provide the tracking action for the sliding table.

—VANESSA SKEDZIELEWSKI, *Sierra Madre, Calif.*

Masking-Tape Drill Stop

THE BEST DEPTH STOP for a portable electric drill is a masking-tape flag around the bit stem, as shown in the drawing below. Masking tape works on all kinds of bits, is easy to set to the right depth, and never mars the workpiece. The advantage of the flag is that you don't have to strain your eyes to tell when the tape reaches the surface—you simply stop drilling when the flag sweeps the chips away.

—RICHARD R. KRUEGER, *Seattle, Wash.,*
and Norman Crowfoot, Pinetop, Ariz.

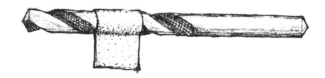

Horizontal Boring Jig for Turned Posts

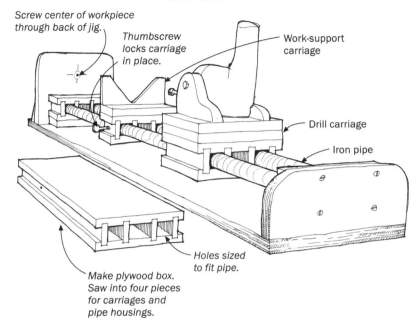

Screw center of workpiece through back of jig.

Thumbscrew locks carriage in place.

Work-support carriage

Drill carriage

Iron pipe

Holes sized to fit pipe.

Make plywood box. Saw into four pieces for carriages and pipe housings.

I WAS RECENTLY FACED WITH the challenge of drilling precisely centered holes along the centerline axis of some turned posts. Because the bed of my lathe wasn't long enough to accommodate the posts, I built a horizontal boring jig using plywood scraps and common iron pipe.

The jig consists of a bed and two carriages, one for the drill and another for supporting the work. First I glued up a hollow plywood box, 16 in. long, with three compartments running the full length. I routed grooves for the vertical walls into the top and bottom of the box. Then I carefully spaced and sized the plywood pieces so that the iron pipe would fit snugly in the openings. Later, I cut this box into four sections to make the two carriages and two pipe housings in the bed.

I wanted to be able to lock the work-support carriage in place to the pipe bed, so I drilled holes and installed T-nuts in the walls of the box before gluing it up. After the glue had cured, I cut the 16-in. box into four sections—two longer sections for the carriages and two shorter sections for the pipe housings in the bed.

I added spacer blocks to the top of the drill carriage to raise up and support the drill. I took advantage of the holes tapped into each side of the drill handle to screw the drill in place on top of the carriage. By adjusting the drill in place with shims, I was able to get it set to cut holes perfectly centered into one end of the turned posts. I also drilled a small pilot hole through the back of the boring jig for a screw to hold the other end of the workpiece steady.

—G. M. WILLIAMS, *Newport News, Va.*

Drilling Table Pins

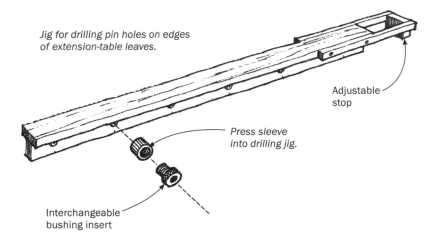

Jig for drilling pin holes on edges
of extension-table leaves.

Adjustable stop

Press sleeve
into drilling jig.

Interchangeable
bushing insert

F OR YEARS I USED a doweling jig to drill holes for pins in extension tables and leaves. This approach, unfortunately, requires dozens of separate operations, each subject to error or misalignment. So I came up with a jig that allows me to drill all the holes on each side of a table part in perfect alignment.

The jig is simply a wooden T-beam containing precisely spaced bushings. My jig is 48 in. long with bushings set 9 in. apart. I use two-part drill bushings that consist of a sleeve and a bushing insert (available in various sizes), which threads into the sleeve. Sleeves and bushings are available from Rockler Woodworking and Hardware (4365 Willow Dr., Medina, MN 55340; 800-279-4441). The jig, fitted with an adjustable stop on one end, can be centered on different-sized tabletops.

To use the jig, I lay out the tabletop halves and any leaves in their correct positions. Then I mark one end of all parts with an X. This is the reference end that I hook the jig's stop against. I clamp the jig into place, screw appropriately sized drill bushings into the sleeves on the exposed side of the jig, and drill the holes. I move the jig to each leaf and drill all the edges in the same way. These are the holes for the pins. To drill matching pin holes in the corresponding leaves, I remove the drill bushings and screw them into the sleeves from the opposite side of the jig.

To make the traditional wooden pins, I use ⅜-in. dowel stock cut to 1-in. lengths. To keep them from binding in the pin holes, I mount the pins in a three-jaw chuck on the lathe and sand down half the length and round the ends. You can also use brass pins (⅜-in.-dia. brass pins that fit the sleeves require ⅜₆ in. dia. holes). The pins are also available from Rockler.

—CHRIS BECKSVOORT, *New Gloucester, Maine*

Modifying Twist Drills for Wood

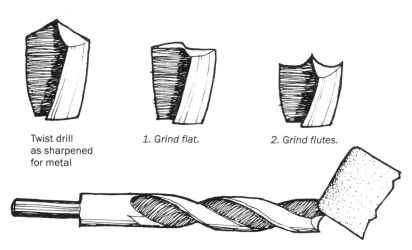

Twist drill
as sharpened
for metal

1. Grind flat.

2. Grind flutes.

Grind flutes with corner of grind-
stone or with cone-shaped stone.

A WORN-OUT TWIST DRILL can be modified to perform much better in wood. First grind the tip flat. Then, using a cone-shaped stone in a hobby grinder or the rounded-over corner of an abrasive wheel, grind two hollows—one on each side of the center. The hollows form a center spur and two outer spurs. Be sure to bevel the hollows so that the back side of the flutes will clear the wood.

In use, the center spur holds the bit stable and keeps it from wandering. The outer spurs cut the wood's fibers in advance of the cutting edge to give straight, clean holes.

—STANLEY F. KAYES, *Richmond, Va.*

Modifying Drill Bits for Brass

HERE'S A TIP WELL known in the metalworking field, but perhaps not common knowledge among woodworkers. When drilling soft metals such as brass, always grind or stone a small flat on the bit's cutting edge. This flat prevents the drill from chattering and results in much cleaner drilling.

—THOMAS J. TIDD, *Springfield, Pa.*

Flat

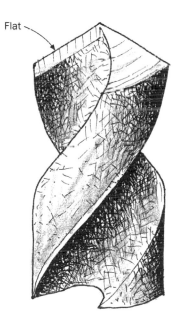

Drilling Long Holes

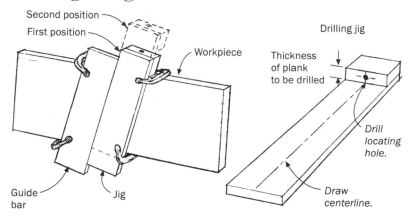

Second position

First position

Drilling jig

Workpiece

Thickness of plank to be drilled

Guide bar

Jig

Drill locating hole.

Draw centerline.

D RILLING A LONG, ACCURATE hole, from edge to edge across the width of a board, for example, is one of the few procedures in woodworking that really requires assistance from jigs and guides.

To bore an accurate hole through the width of a plank, I make a jig. If the drill-locating hole in the jig is accurately bored (a drill press helps), I can't miss. For this job, I prefer "aircraft bits," which are long twist drills with a shank that has the same diameter as the bit.

On the plank, mark the line you want the hole to follow and clamp the guide bar parallel to it. Then clamp the jig against the guide bar as shown, with the drill-bit holder against the edge of the plank, and bore a shallow hole in the edge of the plank. Unclamp the jig, slide it along the guide bar so that the drill-locating end moves away from the edge of the board, and reclamp, keeping the jig against the guide bar. Now, the drill bit will be supported farther back along its shank. Bore halfway through the plank, then flip the jig end-for-end without changing the position of the guide bar, and repeat the procedure on the other edge of the board.

—MIKE PODMANICZKY, *Thomaston, Maine, from a question by Lazlo Spectrum, Tucson, Ariz.*

Bicycle Tube Drill Chuck Aid

CUT A LENGTH OF bicycle inner tube an inch or two long and stretch it over the middle part of your drill chuck. The rubber will make it much easier to spin the chuck open and closed by hand.

—BILL WEBSTER, *Chillicothe, Ill.*

Shopmade Counterbore

HERE IS AN EASILY made counterbore for bolt heads, nuts, and washers. With it you can avoid the problem of centering a second bit over a previously drilled bolt hole. Make the tool from a length of steel rod the same size as your bolt stock. Find a flat washer that just slips on the rod, saw a slot in it, and twist the washer apart slightly. Weld the washer to the rod about 1 in. from one end with the lower edge of the split facing clockwise. File the pilot end of the rod for proper clearance and sharpen the cutting edge of the washer with a file.

—CARL MEINZINGER, *Guemes Island, Wash.*

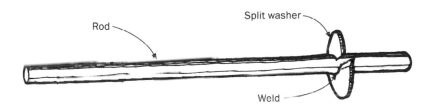

Rod

Split washer

Weld

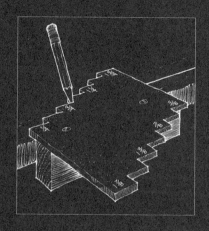

MEASURING, MARKING & LAYOUT

Improved Marking Gauge Point

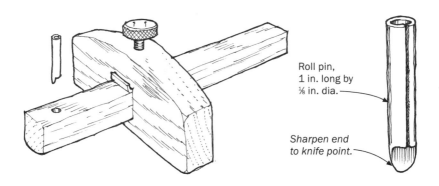

Roll pin,
1 in. long by
⅛ in. dia.

Sharpen end
to knife point.

H ERE'S A MARKING GAUGE point that has several advantages: It leaves a knife-clean line, and its depth and angle to the marking gauge fence are easily adjusted.

Start with a 1-in.-long, ⅛-in.-dia. roll pin, available at your local hardware or auto-parts store. The spring-steel pins, made to fit tightly in a hole, will really hold an edge. Grind or file away one end of the pin, leaving a knife-like nib as shown. Orient the nib opposite the slot in the roll pin. If grinding, dip the pin in water frequently to keep it from losing its temper, before you hone the nib on a whetstone. Install the pin in a properly sized hole through the marking gauge arm. Using a wooden block, press the pin in a short amount. Then, with pliers, angle the nib slightly so that it will pull the work into the fence when used. Press the pin in until only ⅛ in. of the blade is exposed.

When properly honed and installed, the new pin in your gauge will mark a clean line across the grain, even on open-pored wood like red oak, without splintering or tearing.

—RICH HAENDEL, *Iowa City, Iowa*

Marking-Gauge Locking Device

MANY OF US MAKE marking gauges and other tools that require a beam to be locked where it slides through the fence. A wedge can be used, but a screw is more positive and more accurate. Of course, screws with wooden threads are nice, but the means for cutting them are uncommon in the average tool kit. So here is an alternate. The version shown in the sketch below is a panel gauge with its fence notched to ride the edges of large panels. This raises the beam above the surface of the panel, cutting down friction and increasing accuracy.

For the screw, you need nothing more than an ordinary ⅜-in. bolt with a square nut. Cut a slot above the beam mortise into which the square nut will slide and be captured. Also enlarge the mortise to allow enough clearance for a pressure pad bent up from ¼₆-in.-thick brass. Bend up the ends of the pressure pad height enough to hide the ends of the nut slot. To complete the gauge, drill a hole for the bolt down from the top of the stock into the nut-capturing slot. You may wish to install a ¼₆-in. rod through the head of the bolt so it can be tightened without a wrench.

—PERCY W. BLANDFORD, *Stratford-upon-Avon, England*

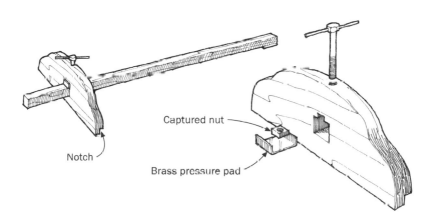

Captured nut

Notch

Brass pressure pad

Preset Mortise Gauge

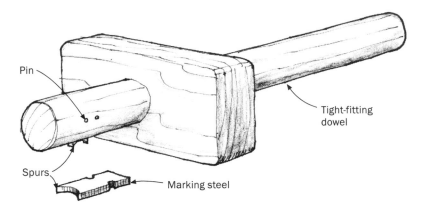

Pin

Tight-fitting dowel

Spurs

Marking steel

I SPECIALIZE IN MAKING CHAIRS, and after a few years I realized that my mortise-and-tenon joints were all just about the same thickness, ⅜ in. To save the time spent setting up my adjustable mortise gauge, I made one with a fixed ⅜-in. setting. The most important component is a piece of 1/16-in.-thick steel ground exactly ⅜ in. wide and shaped as shown, which provides two marking spurs. The steel should always be sharpened on the inside hollow so the outside dimension is not altered.

Fasten the marking steel into a slot in the dowel with rivets or a small wedge. The dowel should be a hard, stiff piece of wood such as oak. I made the body of the gauge from hornbeam, a dense but non-brittle wood. I omitted the usual wedge for locking the gauge at its setting because the dowel fit so tightly into the body. To adjust the gauge, I tap the dowel with a small hammer.

—STEFAN DURING, *Texel, Holland*

Marking Dark Woods with a White Charcoal Pencil

WHEN TRACING A PATTERN ON dark wood, such as walnut, use a charcoal white pencil available at your local artist-supply store.

— JOSEPH M. HERRMANN, *Jefferson, Ohio*

Double-Duty Marking Gauge

TO DOUBLE THE USEFULNESS of a marking gauge, install a pencil in a screw-tightened hole at the unused end. There are many situations where a pencil line is preferable to a scratch. One can also put an india-ink drafting pen in the hole and draw nice smooth lines parallel to an edge they look very much like ebony inlay.

—SIMON A. WATTS, *San Francisco, Calif.*

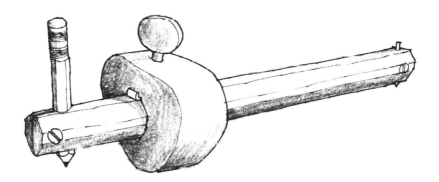

Overhang Marking Gauge

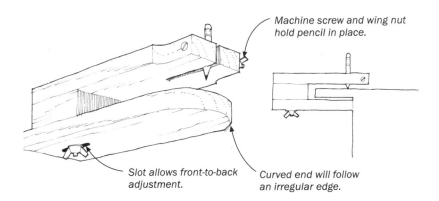

Machine screw and wing nut hold pencil in place.

Slot allows front-to-back adjustment.

Curved end will follow an irregular edge.

ORIGINALLY, I MADE THIS jig to mark some laminate slightly over-sized for trimming. Then I realized how handy the jig would be for other tasks, like marking a cutting line on the edges of an irregular deck. For a one-time job, it's easy to make up a jig with a few scraps held together by a C-clamp. Or, you can make a more permanent adjustable version, as shown in the drawing above.

—LEON G. WILDE, *Andover, Mass.*

Making Pencil Lines Visible with Chalk

ON DARK WOODS, SUCH as walnut, go over your pencil line with chalk. The chalk will adhere to the wood, not to the graphite, resulting in a black-on-white line that's easy to see.

—E. S. MARTIN, *Montrose, Ala.*

Trammel Heads for Occasional Use

FACED WITH THE OCCASIONAL need to draw large-radius circles, I made a pair of wooden trammel heads that will fit on any available scrap 1x2.

Each head is 1¾ in. square in section, with a notch to accept the beam and a wedge for tightening. A clamping block at the bottom of each head will take a steel spike or a pencil. To make the clamping block, drill a ⅚-in. hole in the center of the bottom, then cut away a portion of the head halfway through the hole. Drill the block for two tightening screws.

—PERCY W. BLANDFORD, *Stratford-upon-Avon, England*

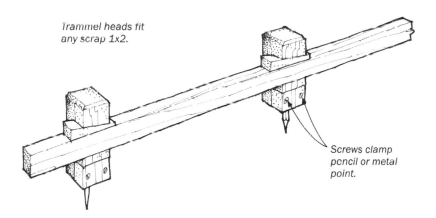

Trammel heads fit any scrap 1x2.

Screws clamp pencil or metal point.

Standard Pencil Gauge

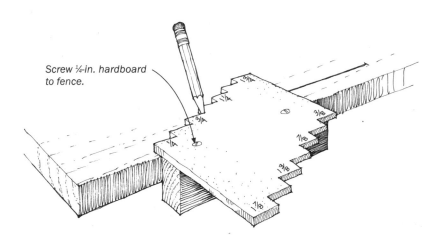

Screw ¼-in. hardboard to fence.

I N CABINETRY, THERE ARE many occasions when you need to mark distances from an edge and some of these recur frequently. This gauge allows you to mark distances from the edge of stock by drawing with a pencil in the appropriate notch.

The example shown above is made from ¼-in. hardboard screwed to a piece of ¾-in. square stock. It has notches at ¼-in. intervals on one side and intermediate ⅛-in. spacings on the other, but you can arrange notches and the size of the gauge to suit your needs.

—PERCY W. BLANDFORD, *Stratford-upon-Avon, England*

Guide for Drawing Parallel Lines

ERE IS A TOOL used by old-time patternmakers and draftsmen to
lay out parallel lines. Strangely enough, I don't think this tool
was ever commercially available; the old craftsmen just made their
own. The tool is simply a flat, 1-in.- to 2-in.-dia. steel, aluminum, or
brass disc with ¹⁄₁₆-in.-dia. holes drilled around the edge. The space
between each hole and the edge of the disc determines the distance
between the drawn line and the fence guiding the disc. I bored
my holes in from the edge at points that mark the decimal equivalents
of fractions commonly used in woodworking. The ¹⁄₁₆-in.-dia. holes
are just large enough to accommodate a scribe point or sharp
pencil point.

—DEVORE O. BURCH, *Fort Worth, Tex.*

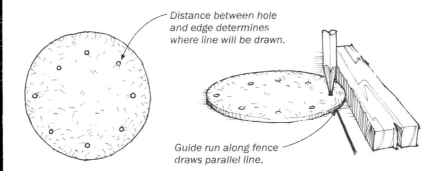

Distance between hole
and edge determines
where line will be drawn.

Guide run along fence
draws parallel line.

Picture-Frame Marking Fixture Is Adjustable

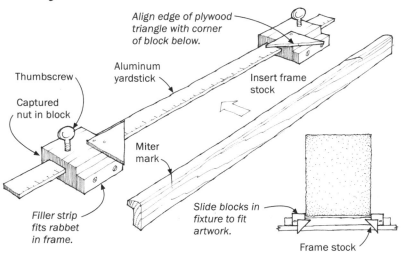

Align edge of plywood triangle with corner of block below.

Aluminum yardstick

Insert frame stock

Thumbscrew

Captured nut in block

Miter mark

Filler strip fits rabbet in frame.

Slide blocks in fixture to fit artwork.

Frame stock

WHEN I HAD TO make a large number of hardwood picture frames, I designed this fixture to help me mark out miter lines on the frame stock. The fixture, which adjusts to fit the artwork you're framing, consists of an aluminum yardstick and two shop-built sliding blocks. Each is equipped with a thumbscrew for locking a 45° thin-plywood triangle to mark the miters and a replaceable filler strip cut to fit the rabbet in the frame. It's important to align the edge of the triangle over the corner of the block below for proper registration.

To use, adjust the sliding blocks to touch each edge of the artwork, and lock the blocks into position with the thumbscrews. Place the frame stock in the jig, so the rabbet fits over the filler strip, and adjust the stock position until you have the grain pattern you want. Now mark the miter line on both ends of the frame by scribing against the triangle.

—WARREN BENDER, *Medford, N.Y.*

Dressmaker's Tape Is Handy in the Shop

A CLOTH DRESSMAKER'S TAPE, available from any sewing store (or swiped from a nearby household sewing machine), is a good addition to the woodworking shop. Use it for measuring those curved items that defy a metal tape. When necessary, attach it with masking tape. To find centers, just fold the tape in half.

—ROGER RUSSELL, *Anderson Island, Wash.*

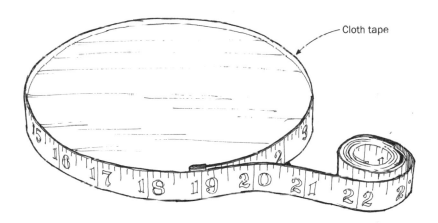

Cloth tape

Center Finders —
Three Variations on a Theme

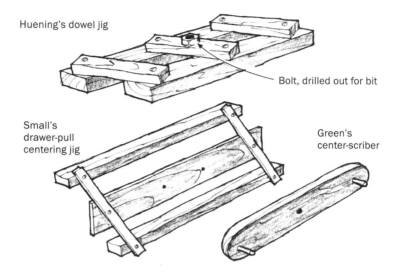

Huening's dowel jig

Bolt, drilled out for bit

Small's
drawer-pull
centering jig

Green's
center-scriber

A N OLD ORGAN-BUILDER friend showed me this handy home-
made guide for center-drilling holes in the edges of boards to
be doweled and edge-glued. The device consists of five sticks of hardwood screwed together in the configuration shown in the top
illustration above.

The sticks should pivot so that the device collapses like a parallelo-
gram. For the drill guide, fit the center strip with a bolt ⅛ in. larger
than the bit size. Then, using a drill press for accuracy, drill a pilot hole
through the bolt using a bit one number larger than the bit you
intend to use for doweling. To use, first align the edges of the boards
and mark off the dowel locations with a square. To center the dowels,
set the device to straddle each board's edge and squeeze the parallelo-
gram shut. Then slide the device to each mark, and drill.

—JOHN HUENING, *Seffner, Fla.*

HERE'S A SELF-CENTERING jig for boring drawer-pull holes (see the bottom left illustration on the facing page). The pivoting sticks should be made long enough to span your widest drawer. The center plate may be fitted with drill-bit guide bushings or just small holes for marking with an awl.

—J. B. SMALL, *Newville, Pa.*

THE OLD-TIME GADGET shown in the bottom right illustration on the facing page is handy for center-scribing boards. Install dowel pegs at the ends of the device and drill a hole in the center for a pencil point.

—LARRY GREEN, *Bethel, Conn.*

Shims from Playing Cards

WE USE PLAYING CARDS for shims when making fine adjustments on setups and jigs. "Bicycle" brand cards are 0.011 in. thick—you can bet on it.

—EDWARD F. GROH, *Napierville, Ill.*,
and Charles E. Cohn, Clarendon Hills, Ill.

Dividing a Circle into Equidistant Intervals

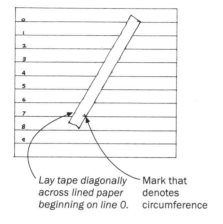

Lay tape diagonally across lined paper beginning on line 0. Mark that denotes circumference

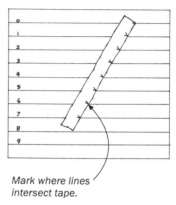

Mark where lines intersect tape.

H ERE'S HOW TO DIVIDE the circumference of a disc into equally spaced intervals. First, draw a series of parallel equidistant lines across a large sheet of paper. The distance between the lines should be slightly less than the smallest interval you will normally use. Number the lines starting with line 0, 1, 2, 3, and so on. Now wrap a length of tape around the disc, mark where the ends overlap, and remove the tape. Assuming the number of desired intervals is seven, for example, you would lay the tape diagonally across the sheet so that line 0 intersects one end of the tape and line 7 intersects the mark denoting the circumference. Now mark where each intermediate line intersects your tape for accurate equidistant intervals without measuring. Rewrap the tape around the disc and transfer the marks from the tape to the disc.

—KATHLEEN WISSINGER, *Elkton, Va.*

Scribing Large Circles

H ERE'S AN INEXPENSIVE AND easy-to-make alternative to trammel
points for scribing large circles or arcs. First cut a long hardwood beam to fit the hole in your marking gauge. Make a vertical
sawcut in one end of the beam, and drill a ½-in. hole through the cut
to hold a pencil. Now, drive a brad in the bottom of the gauge to
serve as a compass point, install the beam in the gauge block, and
you're ready to scribe a circle as big as the beam.

—GREGORY V. TOLMAN, *Evergreen, Colo.*

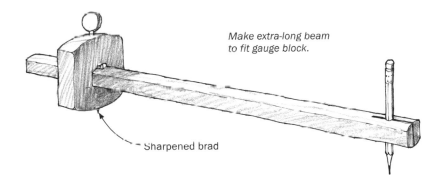

Make extra-long beam
to fit gauge block.

Sharpened brad

Circle Division Table

D URING MY 40 YEARS as a modelmaker, I have used this circle division table many times. I know of no faster method to divide a circle into several equal parts. To use the table, just pick the number of divisions you want from the "No. of spaces" column. Multiply the selected "Length of chord" times the diameter of your circle and set a divider to this reading. Then simply walk the dividers around the circle, marking each point. If you're working with small circles, it helps to have a rule divided in hundredths to set the dividers accurately.

These figures are for a 1-in.-dia. circle. For other sizes, multiply the length of chord by the diameter of the circle desired.

—RAY ELAM, *Los Gatos, Calif.*

No. of spaces	Length of chord	No. of spaces	Length of chord	No. of spaces	Length of chord	No. of spaces	Length of chord
3	0.8660	28	0.1120	53	0.0592	78	0.0403
4	0.7071	29	0.1081	54	0.0581	79	0.0398
5	0.5878	30	0.1045	55	0.0571	80	0.0393
6	0.5000	31	0.1012	56	0.0561	81	0.0388
7	0.4339	32	0.0980	57	0.0551	82	0.0383
8	0.3827	33	0.0951	58	0.0541	83	0.0378
9	0.3420	34	0.0923	59	0.0532	84	0.0374
10	0.3090	35	0.0896	60	0.0523	85	0.0370
11	0.2818	36	0.0872	61	0.0515	86	0.0365
12	0.2588	37	0.0848	62	0.0507	87	0.0361
13	0.2393	38	0.0826	63	0.0499	88	0.0357
14	0.2224	39	0.0805	64	0.0491	89	0.0353
15	0.2079	40	0.0785	65	0.0483	90	0.0349
16	0.1951	41	0.0765	66	0.0476	91	0.0345
17	0.1837	42	0.0747	67	0.0469	92	0.0341
18	0.1736	43	0.0730	68	0.0462	93	0.0338
19	0.1645	44	0.0713	69	0.0455	94	0.0334
20	0.1564	45	0.0698	70	0.0449	95	0.0331
21	0.1490	46	0.0682	71	0.0442	96	0.0327
22	0.1423	47	0.0668	72	0.0436	97	0.0324
23	0.1362	48	0.0654	73	0.0430	98	0.0321
24	0.1305	49	0.0641	74	0.0424	99	0.0317
25	0.1253	50	0.0628	75	0.0419	100	0.0314
26	0.1205	51	0.0616	76	0.0413		
27	0.1161	52	0.0604	77	0.0408		

Drawing a Half-Ellipse

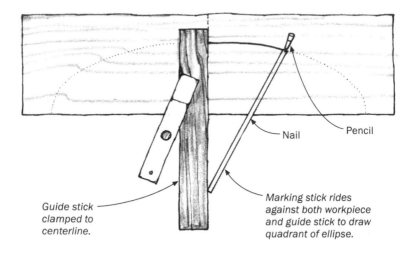

Nail

Pencil

Guide stick clamped to centerline.

Marking stick rides against both workpiece and guide stick to draw quadrant of ellipse.

W E USE THIS METHOD to draw half-ellipses for laying out seat backs in our shop. First, mark the rise and run of the half-ellipse on the stock and clamp a 1x2 guide stick on the centerline, as shown in the sketch above. Now cut a 1x1 marking stick half as long as the ellipse and notch one end to hold a pencil point. Drive a nail through the stick at a distance from the notched end equal to the rise of the ellipse. To draw the ellipse, hold a pencil in the notch. Move the head of the stick from left to right while riding the nail against the stock and the tail of the stick against the guide stick. Reclamp the guide stick to the other side of the centerline to complete the curve.

—DOUG HANSEN, *Letcher, S.D.*

Draftsman's Method for Drawing an Ellipse

WHEN LAYING OUT AN ellipse, most people care more about its finished length and width than about the distance between the two focal points. The draftsman's method shown in the sketch below gets directly to the point without requiring calculations and gadgets.

—LAWRENCE WHYTOCK, *Brockville, Ont., Canada*

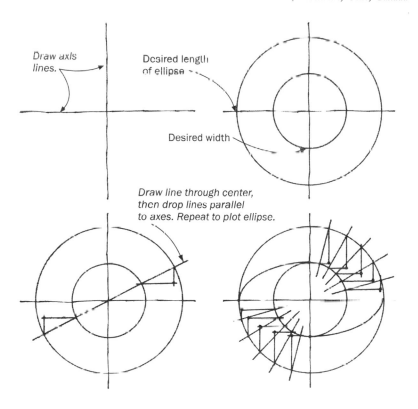

Draw axis lines.

Desired length of ellipse

Desired width

Draw line through center, then drop lines parallel to axes. Repeat to plot ellipse.

Ellipse Drawing Aid

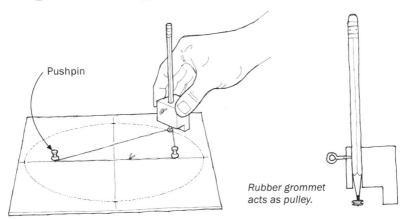

Pushpin

Rubber grommet
acts as pulley.

H ERE'S A SIMPLE LITTLE device that makes drawing an ellipse easier and more accurate. To lay out the ellipse, first draw the vertical and horizontal dimensions of the ellipse on a pattern board. Now
drive two pushpins into the pattern material along the long axis of the
ellipse. Tie a loop of string loosely around the pins, as shown above.
After some trial and error, you should be able to vary the position of
the pushpins and the length of the loop so that the string, when taut,
touches the vertical and horizontal dimensions of the ellipse.

Now you're ready to use the drawing device. Mount a pencil in the
device, catch the pencil in the loop and, keeping the loop taut, trace
the circumference to draw the ellipse. The device will keep the pencil
perpendicular to the paper, which is hard to do without assistance. Use
a screw eye to lock the pencil at the right height. To keep the string
taut and down near the surface, place a small rubber grommet, available from auto-parts stores, on the tip of the pencil. The string will
ride in the groove of the grommet as you move the pencil.

—ROBERT J. GABOR, *Pittsboro, N.C.*

Framing-Square Calipers

THIS MAY BE AN OLD trick, but I thought of it myself and was smiling the rest of the workday. My spring calipers measure only up to 6 in. One day, I needed an exact measurement of a wooden column that was several inches larger than that. It occurred to me that I had two small framing squares the same size. I mated the bodies together, as shown in the sketch below, and took the measurement where the tongue of one square intersected the interior scale of the other one.

—MARK DICHIARA, *Atlanta, Ga.*

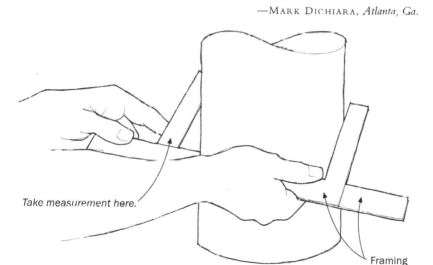

Take measurement here.

Framing squares

Parabola Marker

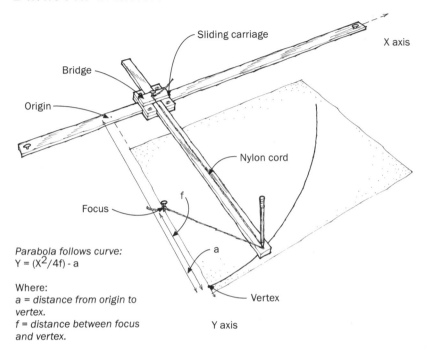

Sliding carriage

X axis

Bridge

Origin

Nylon cord

Focus

f

Parabola follows curve:
$Y = (X^2/4f) - a$

a

Where:
a = distance from origin to vertex.
f = distance between focus and vertex.

Vertex

Y axis

T HIS DEVICE, WHICH TRACES a portion of a parabola, is a simplified version of one developed by Terry Soper of Lockheed Engineering and Management Services Co. and published in the NASA Tech Briefs. It's just as useful for laying out parabolic shapes for boat or furniture construction as it is for designing parabolic antennae.

The marker consists of just a few parts: two tracks, a sliding carriage, and a piece of nylon cord. For small parabolas, I recommend maple splints about ⅜ in. thick and 1 in. wide for the wooden parts. Make the carriage by screwing together four pieces of wood into a simple lapped frame, as shown in the sketch. You want both tracks to slide smoothly through the carriage but to remain at right angles to each other. Attach a small wooden bridge over the top of the carriage, as shown, to anchor one end of the cord.

To use the device, first draw the Y axis, representing the parabola's centerline, and the X axis, which will be the stationary track's location. Next, locate two points along the Y axis: the focus, at the "center" of the parabola, and the vertex, at the bottom of the parabola. If you know the exact mathematical shape you want, use the formula shown to establish the focus and vertex.

Or you can use trial and error to establish these points by keeping this relationship in mind: the nearer the stationary track is to the focus, the deeper the parabola, the farther away the track is from the focus, the shallower the parabola. Attach the cord to a nail driven at the focus, and then with the moveable track slid up to the focus and the pencil point at the vertex, loop the cord around the pencil and back to the bridge on the carriage. The string should just be long enough to let the pencil touch the vertex. Now start sliding the carriage along the stationary track while pulling on the moveable track to keep the string taut. The pencil will scribe a perfect parabola.

—JIM McGILL, *Seattle, Wash.*

Laying Out Cams with String

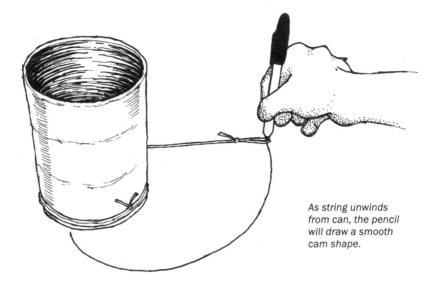

As string unwinds
from can, the pencil
will draw a smooth
cam shape.

T HE EASIEST WAY TO draw a cam is to use the unwinding string
principle—tie a string around a cylinder of suitable size to create
the desired cam shape. Aluminum food cans are often about the right
size. First, tie a length of string around the can, and tie a loop in the
end of the string. Then wind the string fully around the cylinder, and
place a pencil in the loop with the point where the cam is to begin.
Unwind the string by moving the pencil away from the cylinder. The
point of the pencil will scribe a cam that expands in proportion to the
diameter of the cylinder. Because the distance from the center of the
cam increases at a constant rate, the resulting cam will have a smooth
and controlled action.

—E. W. CARSON, *Blacksburg, Va.*

Adjustable Curve

T O MAKE THIS ADJUSTABLE curve, start with a piece of fine, straightgrained hardwood—hickory is best. Cut a ¼-in.-thick strip about 36 in. long and 1½ in. wide. Now taper the strip to ¾ in. wide and ½₂ in. thick at one end. Glue a reinforcing patch on the thin end and saw a small notch in each end of the piece. To complete the curve, tie a series of knots in a string and string up the curve like a bow. Unstring the curve when it's not in use.

—FLOYD LIEN, *Aptos, Calif.*

Tapered hickory bow

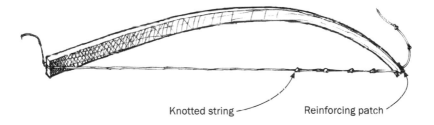

Knotted string 　　　　　Reinforcing patch

Drawing Large Shallow Curves

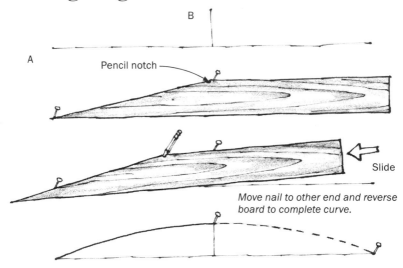

WHEN I WAS A BOATBUILDER we used this shallow-curve drawing method to set out the deck beams of yachts. The trick works for drawing any such curve with a known rise and run.

You'll need two nails and a "spile board." Cut the spile board as wide as the curve's rise and taper the board on one end with the length of the taper equal to the curve's run. Notch the board at the location shown above to catch a pencil point.

Drive one nail at point A and another at point B. With a pencil in the notch and the spile board positioned as shown in the sketch, slide the board toward the nail at A to draw the curve. Nail A can be removed and driven in the other end to complete the curve. In our situation, the method was used to make a template from which all the shorter beams and carlings could be marked.

—ERNIE IVES, *Sproughton, Ipswich, England*

Drawing a Curve with a Spline

D RAWING A CURVE WITH a thin wooden spline is an awkward task for one person to do. You really need one pair of hands to hold the spline steady and another pair to draw the curve. Here's how to draw a curve without having to search for a helper.

Rip a ³⁄₃₂-in.-thick spline from ¾-in., knot-free stock, about 6 in. longer than the curve you want to draw. Mark the centerline on the spline. Make two stop blocks out of scrap stock. Mark the two end points and the middle apex point of the desired curve on the workpiece, and attach the two stop blocks at the end points with hot-melt glue. With one hand, place the spline against the two blocks, and push it up, aligning the center mark with the apex mark on the workpiece. Draw the curve with the other hand.

—JOHN SAGGIO, *Little Neck, N.Y.*

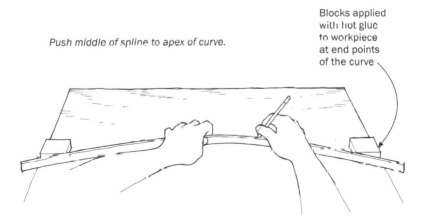

Push middle of spline to apex of curve.

Blocks applied
with hot glue
to workpiece
at end points
of the curve

Calculating the Radius of an Arc

Desired width, A

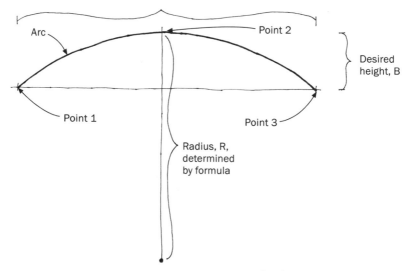

QUITE OFTEN, WHEN DESIGNING a curved cabinet or tabletop, you need to determine the radius of an arc that will give you a specific amount of convexity (height of arc) and also fit within a specified width. Here's a formula for calculating the radius of an arc that must pass through three predetermined points. With it you can find the radius (R) from the desired width (A) and height (B) as defined by the three points, shown below. The formula is:

$$R = \frac{(A/2)^2 + B^2}{2B}$$

For example, to find the radius of an arc that is 12 in. wide and 2 in. high, let A = 12 and B = 2. Then:

$$R = \frac{(12/2)^2 + 2^2}{2 \times 2}$$

$$R = \frac{36 + 4}{4}$$

Finally, R = 10. The arc's radius is 10 in.

—BARRIE GRAHAM, *Arundel, Que., Canada*

Using Washers for Drawing Curves

I KEEP A STOCK OF WASHERS in many sizes to use as templates when drawing rounded corners. Buy one washer of every size from the hardware store, and hang them on a nail in your shop. For larger curves, use jar lids and paint can lids. They're all true circles and less trouble to use than a compass when only part of a circle is needed.

—PERCY BLANDFORD, *Stratford-upon-Avon, England*

Keep stack of different-sized washers for drawing arcs and rounding corners.

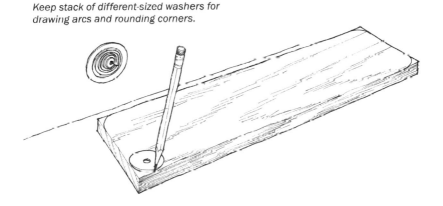

Sliding Measuring Sticks

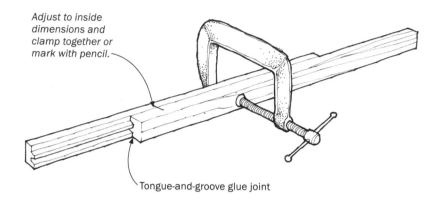

Adjust to inside
dimensions and
clamp together or
mark with pencil.

Tongue-and-groove glue joint

T HE NEXT TIME YOU'RE running tongue-and-groove glue joints,
rip off some sticks about ⅜ in. thick, with the joint profile on
one side. Put the two sticks together to make a sliding measuring
stick that can take inside measurements accurately. The measurements
can be registered by marking across both sticks with a pencil or by
clamping the two sticks together with a small C-clamp. The measuring
stick is especially useful for checking a door opening for consistent
width from top to bottom.

—ROBERT M. VAUGHAN, *Roanoke, Va.*

Approximating Angles

HERE'S A SURPRISINGLY ACCURATE procedure to estimate angles using only a rule and a compass. First, draw a circle with a radius of 5¾ in. Let's assume you want a 10° angle. Mark off two points 1 in. apart (a 1-in. chord) on the circumference. Join the two points with the center of the circle, and the resulting angle is almost exactly 10°. If you want 20°, just lay out two 1-in. chords (not one 2-in. chord). For angles less than 10°, use fractions of an inch or just split the distance by eye. For large angles, lay out multiples of 60° (using the compass set to the circle's radius) then add or subtract 1-in. (10°) slices to get the angle you want.

—JULES PAQUIN, *Laval, Que., Canada*

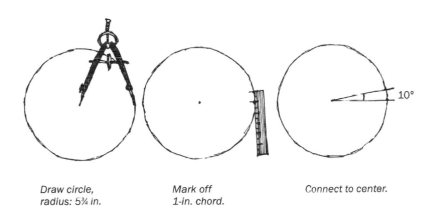

Draw circle,
radius: 5¾ in.

Mark off
1-in. chord.

Connect to center.

10°

Octagon Marking Gauge

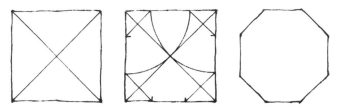

Scribe diagonals; then compass shows true octagon.

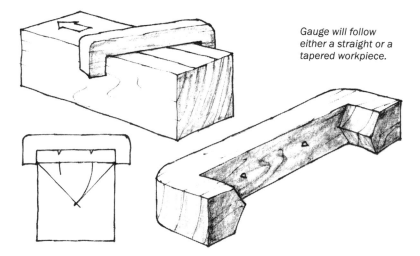

Gauge will follow either a straight or a tapered workpiece.

MANY CRAFTSPEOPLE KNOW THE traditional method for marking a square to make an octagon: First, draw diagonals as shown in the sketch. Then, with a compass set to one-half the diagonal, draw arcs from two corners. Reset the compass and walk it around the square to mark the corners of the octagon.

Repeating this procedure for different-size workpieces can be tedious. This gauge, borrowed from boatbuilding sparmakers, will scratch the lines you need along the length of a square workpiece of any width (less than its capacity), even if the workpiece tapers.

To make the gauge, first cut a cardboard square equal to the largest section you expect to deal with. On the square, draw diagonals and arcs to locate the two scribe points, as shown in the sketch. From a stout piece of hardwood, make a U-shaped gauge body to fit over the cardboard square. Drive nails in the gauge at the proper locations and sharpen. To allow the gauge to be used for smaller work, cut the ears into a prow shape as shown in the drawing.

To mark the square workpiece, angle the gauge until it bears against the sides and draw it along. If the wood tapers, the angle of the gauge will change but the proportions of the spaces across the wood will remain correct.

—PERCY W. BLANDFORD, *Stratford-upon-Avon, England*

Preparing Octagonal Spindle Stock

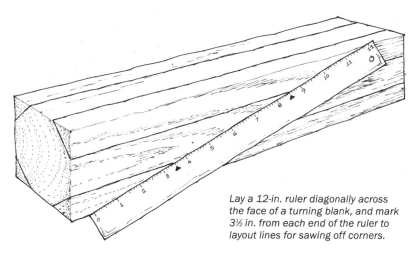

Lay a 12-in. ruler diagonally across
the face of a turning blank, and mark
3½ in. from each end of the ruler to
layout lines for sawing off corners.

HERE IS A QUICK METHOD of marking the amount of corner
stock to be removed from a square blank you want to turn on
a lathe. Simply lay a 12-in. ruler diagonally across the timber, aligning
the zero mark with one edge and the 12-in. mark with the opposite
edge. Then mark points at 3½ in. and 8½ in. Lines drawn through
these points and parallel with the stock's edges will indicate the
amount of stock to be removed to convert the square section into
an octagonal form.

How does this method work? The proportion of 3½ to 12 (or the
easier to work with 7/24) relates to the geometry of an octagon
almost exactly.

—J. H. WALKER, *Aspendale, Victoria, Australia*

Laying Out a Five-Point Star without Math

I'VE READ SEVERAL METHODS for laying out pentagons or five-pointed stars based on algebra or trigonometry. By contrast, my method requires neither calculator, compass, protractor, formulas, nor hard-to-remember constructions. Take a strip of paper as wide as the distance between star points, and carefully tie a simple overhand knot. Thin but strong paper works best. Resist the temptation to flatten and crease the paper until you have removed all the slack. When the strip knot is tight and flattened, you have created a perfect pentagon pattern, as shown in the sketch below. You can scale the pattern up or down to whatever size pentagon you need, or connect the intersections of your paper knot to draw a star.

—RALPH KOEBKE, *Fremont, Ind.*

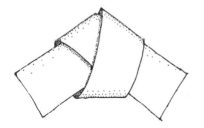

Tie paper strip
in overhand knot.

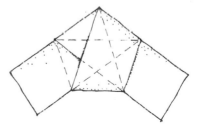

Intersections establish
points of star.

Laying Out a Five-Point Star

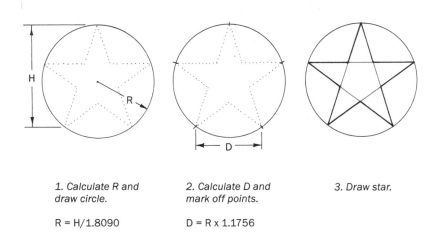

1. Calculate R and draw circle.

R = H/1.8090

2. Calculate D and mark off points.

D = R x 1.1756

3. Draw star.

I RECENTLY NEEDED TO LAY out a symmetrical five-point star. Since using a protractor can be time-consuming, I developed a quick and easy method that allows me to lay out any size star with only a compass and a calculator. To avoid strange fractions in your calculations, you should work in centimeters instead of inches.

To lay out a star of height (H), divide H by 1.8090 to find the radius (R) of the layout circle. Set your compass to R, and draw a circle. Multiply the radius distance by 1.1756 to determine the distance

(D) between the points of the star. Reset your compass to D. Now, start at the top of the circle and move from point to point, marking five equidistant points on the circumference of the circle. To complete the star, connect every other point with a straight line.

For example, if you want a star that's 10cm tall, first determine the radius of the circle using the formula H divided by 1.8090. If the height is 10, then the radius equals 5.5279.

Now, set your compass to 5.5279, and draw a circle before calculating the distance (D) between points. You can determine the distance by multiplying the radius (R) by 1.1756. In this case, D will be 6.4986. Set the compass to 6.4986 and mark out the points of the star.

—DANIEL V. BASS, *Anaheim, Calif.*

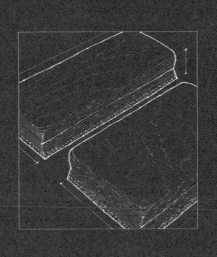

[*Chapter 7*]

SANDING

Sandpaper Cutter

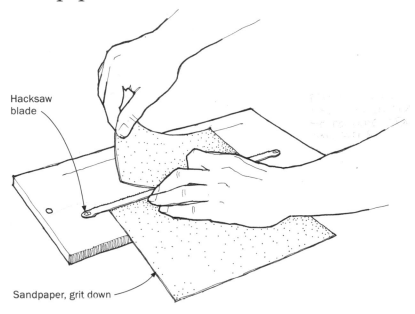

Hacksaw
blade

Sandpaper, grit down

I F YOU'RE LIKE ME, folding and tearing sandpaper along the crease isn't always successful. Instead, try making this simple cutter. Screw an old hacksaw blade to a strip of scrap plywood. Insert a screwdriver under the blade, and twist the screwdriver to provide ample clearance for the sandpaper. To use the cutter, slide the sandpaper, face down, under the blade. When the sandpaper is in position, push the blade down, and pull the sandpaper up. The sandpaper will cut cleanly against the serrated blade.

—ANTHONY GUIDICE, *St. Louis, Mo.*

Sandpaper Sizer

EVERYBODY MAY KNOW THIS one already, but you don't need scissors and a ruler to cut sandpaper to fit your electric sander—just make a sharp-edged wooden strip the size of your sander's paper, place it on the sandpaper, and tear the sheet to size.

—HARRY D. STUMPF, *West Point, N.Y.*

A wooden strip, sized to fit
your electric sander,
saves measuring time.

Sandpaper

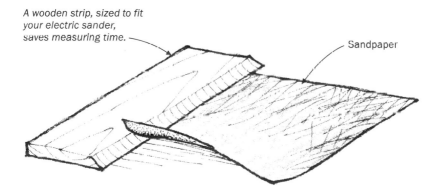

Folding Sandpaper

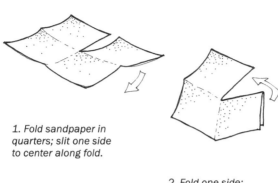

1. Fold sandpaper in quarters; slit one side to center along fold.

2. Fold one side; tuck into opposite crease.

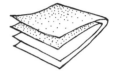

3. Fold so that grit sides do not mate to grit sides. Pad is complete.

H ERE'S A METHOD FOR folding sandpaper that my father, a carpenter, showed me in 1940.

Take a sheet of sandpaper, fold and crease it in half in both directions as though preparing to cut quarter sheets. Cut along any crease, stopping at the center of the sheet. It does not take a rocket scientist to figure out how to fold the sheet so that you don't mate a grit side to a grit side.

—REX HEADLAND, *Pasadena, Newfoundland*

Making a Curved Sanding Block

H ERE IS AN EASY WAY to make a curved sanding block for cove
stock or circular holes. Split a piece of PVC 20 (the lightweight, cheaper stuff) lengthwise on the table saw or bandsaw, so you
have just over a full half cylinder. Size the sandpaper so that it wraps
around the half cylinder with an extra ½-in. flap on both sides. With
the sandpaper in place, snap the block over a length of the next
smaller size pipe to hold the sandpaper in place. Because this works
with any two steps in size, you can vary the radius from ½ in. to 2 in.

—KENNETH E. VINYARD, *Medford, Ore.*

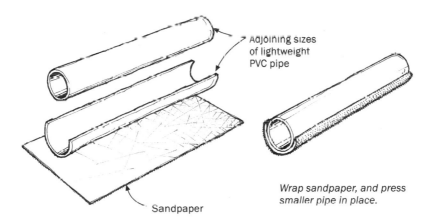

Adjoining sizes
of lightweight
PVC pipe

Sandpaper

Wrap sandpaper, and press
smaller pipe in place.

User-Friendly Sanding Blocks

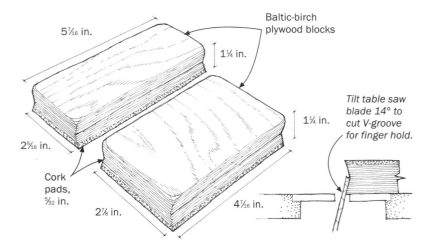

5⁷⁄₁₆ in.

Baltic-birch
plywood blocks

1¼ in.

2⁵⁄₁₆ in.

1¼ in.

Tilt table saw
blade 14° to
cut V-groove
for finger hold.

Cork
pads,
⁵⁄₃₂ in.

2⅞ in.

4⁷⁄₁₆ in.

T O MAKE HAND-SANDING less tiring, our class at Anderson Ranch Arts Center analyzed and redesigned the common sanding block. After experimenting with a variety of materials and thicknesses, the consensus was that a relatively thick (1 in. to 1¼ in.) block laminated from hefty Finply or Baltic-birch plywood is the most comfortable. We glued ⁵⁄₃₂-in.-thick sheet cork, available from any building-supply store, to one side of slightly oversized blanks. Then we trimmed the blocks with the corkside up to reduce tearout.

Opinion was split on whether the blocks should be narrow or wide. To satisfy everyone's ergonomic needs, we came up with the two sizes shown in the drawing above. Each one uses a one-quarter sheet of sandpaper. After the blocks were cut to size, we sliced shallow V-grooves (finger holds) in both long edges of the blocks on the table saw. Finally, we rounded the corners and then lightly sanded all the surfaces.

Our prototypes were reviewed by Nicole Vavuris, a safety engineer
for the city of San Francisco. He said that the stress in the wrists
caused by hand-sanding would be lessened by using these blocks,
which encourage you to sand with the heel of your hand in a "power
grip." Always avoid a fingertip grip.

—JOHN AND CAROLYN GREW-SHERIDAN, *San Francisco, Calif.*
(and the class at Anderson Ranch, Colo.)

Cutting Sandpaper with a Paper Cutter

USE A LEVER-ARM PAPER cutter, available at any office supply
store, to cut sandpaper. The built-in ruler makes the job
simple and quick. Also, the cutter does not get dull quickly, as you
might expect. Mine has been in use for more than five years and still
cuts like new.

—ED REISS, *Berea, Ky.*

Two-Faced Sanding Slab

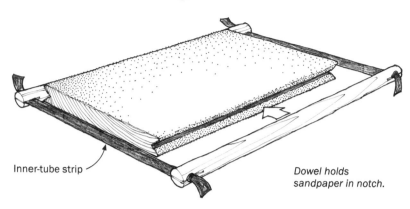

Inner-tube strip

*Dowel holds
sandpaper in notch.*

I SUSPECT MANY AMONG US like to sand small pieces of wood by
rubbing them back and forth on a whole sheet of sandpaper,
finger-pressed against the top of a workbench or the flat table of a
handy woodworking machine. And just as many of us know that it's
only a matter of time before OOPS—we slip and that fresh sheet of
sandpaper is wrinkled or torn. If this sounds familiar, try making this
versatile sanding slab from a piece of scrap and a couple of inner-
tube ribbons. The device firmly clamps a full sheet of sandpaper for
sanding, but allows easy replacement when it's worn out. While you're
at it, make two slabs so you can have four different grades of sandpaper at the ready, simply by flipping the slabs.

Size the slab as long as a sheet of sandpaper but about an inch
narrower so that you can fold the sandpaper's edges over into the
V-grooves and hold them with the tensioned dowels. The thickness of
the slab is not important. No doubt, ¾-in. stock and ¾-in. doweling
would work just fine.

To use the slab, simply fold a sheet of sandpaper over its face, snap the tensioned dowels into the V-grooves, and start sanding. Here's a hint for mounting two sheets at once: Tack two sheets of sandpaper in place temporarily with masking tape before snapping the dowels into the V-grooves.

—FRANK SCHUCH, *La Mesa, Calif.*

Sanding with a Handball Glove

WHEN I HAVE A LOT of power-sanding to do—either finish, belt, or disc—I always wear a handball players' glove. It's ventilated on the back for comfort, and the palm is padded, which helps cushion some of the vibration. I can sand for hours without getting that "tingling" sensation in my hand and arm.

—R. BROBERG, *Huntington Beach, Calif.*

Hand Sander

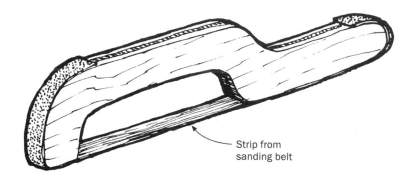

Strip from
sanding belt

H ERE'S AN INEXPENSIVE, quick-to-make hand sander that's effective for smoothing out gouge marks on curved surfaces or for rounding off a sharp edge. You will need some scrap plywood, a used belt from a belt sander, and a little contact cement.

First, cut the plywood into an 8-in.- to 12-in.-long hacksaw shape. Tear a strip from an old sanding belt as wide as the plywood you use and a couple of inches longer than the frame you cut. Spread a little contact cement on the backside of the strip and along the bottom surface of the frame and press the abrasive strip along the bottom of the handle to the front.

When completed, the sander has an open section with a little give for sanding curves and a rigid section for sanding flat surfaces. The rounded ends are designed for sanding concave surfaces. By changing the shape of the frame, the applications are virtually endless. When the abrasive is dull, just pull off the old strip and glue another on.

—RICHARD NEUBAUER JR., *Cincinnati, Ohio*

Long-Lived Sanding Strips

NARROW STRIPS OF SANDPAPER used to sand turnings or curved objects tend to tear, cutting less efficiently as they get shorter until they become just useless pieces of expensive paper. To make them last longer, back them with fiberglass strapping tape; they'll be virtually untearable.

—J. S. GERHSEY, *Lake Ariel, Pa.*

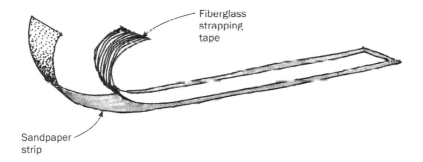

Fiberglass strapping tape

Sandpaper strip

Sanding Concave Surfaces with a Random-Orbit Sander

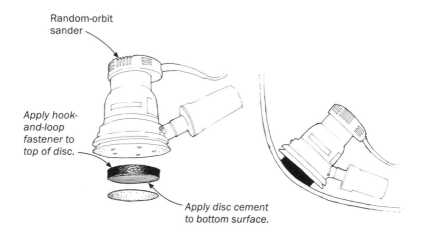

Random-orbit
sander

Apply hook-
and-loop
fastener to
top of disc.

Apply disc cement
to bottom surface.

I LOVE MY RANDOM-ORBIT sander, which removes material fast, is easy to control, and leaves a smooth, uniform surface. When I made a cedar-strip canoe last winter, the random-orbit sander worked like a dream on the outside of the hull, shaping and smoothing the convex curves. On the inside of the hull, however, I was able to use the sander only in some of the flatter areas because the 5-in. pad bridged all but the shallowest concave curves, leaving swirls and gouges at the edges.

After trying a number of solutions, all ineffective, I extended the reach of my sander by adding an auxiliary disc. I cut a 3-in.-dia. disc from ¾-in.-thick neoprene foam and attached a hook-and-loop fastener to one side with polyurethane glue. I sealed the other side with Franklin sanding-disc cement, ending up with something that looked like a Nerf hockey puck. You can buy neoprene pads of different thicknesses at computer-supply stores or by mail order from CGR Products in North Carolina (336-621-4568).

By centering the auxiliary disc on my sander's hook-and-loop pad and using self-stick sandpaper sheets, I was able to reach into almost all of the concave surfaces on the inside of the hull. Smaller discs or softer foams would likely extend the sander's reach to even tighter curves.

Take care in accurately cutting the foam disc and centering it on the sander pad. Any imbalances could result in increased vibration at high speeds, which would be transmitted directly to the user's hands and arms.

—PHILIP JACOBS, *St. Paul, Minn.*

Rubber Fingertips for Sanding

RUBBER FINGERTIPS, AVAILABLE IN several sizes at office supply stores, are ideal finger protectors when a project requires hand-sanding. In addition to saving skin, they help the sandpaper last longer and prevent oily fingerprints on light-colored woods.

—DENNIS SCHORPP, *Monroe, Wash.*

Beltsanding Large Concave Surfaces

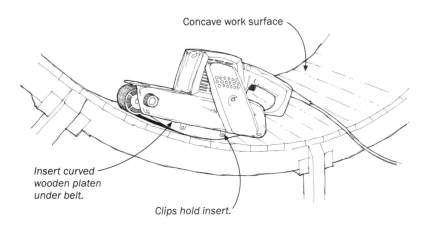

Concave work surface

Insert curved
wooden platen
under belt.

Clips hold insert.

T O BELTS AND LARGE CONCAVE surfaces, make a curved wooden
insert as wide as the sander's platen to go under the belt. Slightly
flatten the insert's crown to get more of the sanding belt in contact
with the surface. There's a limit to the thickness of insert you can use;
you've gone too far if the belt-release mechanism doesn't close properly. The insert should stay in place without any type of attachment. If
it doesn't, use clips to secure the insert.

—CHRIS MARLEY, *Kingston, Jamaica*

Beltsanding Narrow Work

I RECENTLY HAD THE PROBLEM of beltsanding the edge of a 1-in.-thick tabletop. Try as I might, I couldn't help but rock the belt sander. This resulted in a rounded and uneven edge. I solved this problem by clamping a straight length of scrapwood to the tabletop to increase the surface area for the belt sander to rest on. I used a square to make sure the two surfaces were properly aligned, and clamped the scrap piece to the top side of the table to keep from marring it with the clamps.

—ROOPINDER TARA, *Willow Grove, Pa.*

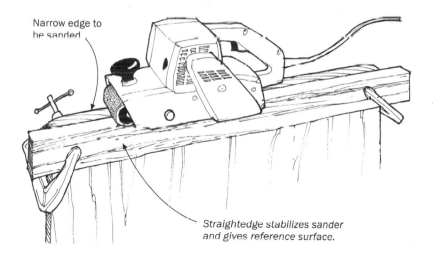

Narrow edge to be sanded

Straightedge stabilizes sander and gives reference surface.

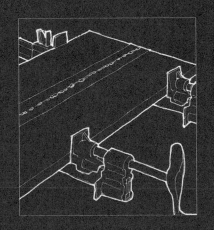

GLUING

Glue Injector

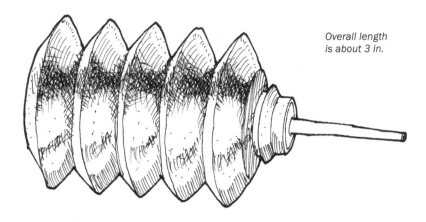

*Overall length
is about 3 in.*

A SK YOUR VETERINARIAN TO save you a few of these little accordion squeeze bottles that come filled with an antiseptic used to irrigate puncture wounds. The bottles make great glue or oil applicators in tight places.

—STEVE ALLARD, *Carbondale, Ill.*

Ultimate Glue Applicator

A PPLYING GLUE TO JOINTS has always been a messy chore, especially when it involves tricky corners or overhead surfaces. This
curved-tip plastic syringe (Monoject #412, available for about 40 cents
from any hospital supply company) solves the problem perfectly. The
tapered, curved tip may be trimmed to handle the viscosity of any
adhesive and allows easy access to all joints. Simply push a pin or nail
into the tip to preserve the adhesive for later use.

—GARY OUWERKERK, *Los Osos, Calif.*

Glue-Mixing Bowl
from a Plastic Soft-Drink Bottle

THE CUT-OFF BOTTOM of a two-liter, plastic, soft-drink bottle makes a perfect mixing bowl for plastic-resin glue and similar compounds. Hardened glue will not stick to the flexible bowl.

—R. S. KJARVAL, *Chicago, Ill.*

No-Mess Epoxy Mixing

TO MIX SMALL AMOUNTS of epoxy, simply squeeze equal amounts of resin and hardener into the corner of a plastic sandwich bag. Twist and mix the two until a uniform color appears. Then puncture the bag with a pin and squeeze out the glue as needed. No clean-up is required—just throw the bag away.

—EDGAR E. GARDNER, *Nashua, N.H.*

Keeping Glue from Sticking to Forms

T O KEEP GLUE FROM sticking to forms and jigs, we use a car wax such as Du Pont Rain Dance or Treewax Four Seasons. Car wax doesn't seem to penetrate and discolor the work the way softer waxes do. Of course, seal the form first with lacquer or shellac.

—PETERMAN LUMBER, *Fontana, Calif.*

Glue Pot Heater

W HILE VISITING LOCAL FURNITURE refinisher Charles Baird, I noticed his novel method of heating a glue pot. He had mounted a common electric iron upside down on a couple of pegs that protruded from the wall, as shown in the drawing above. The glue pot, which sat on the iron's flat surface, was kept at a low, even temperature thanks to the iron's thermostatic control.

—N. CLARKE, *Victoria, B.C., Canada*

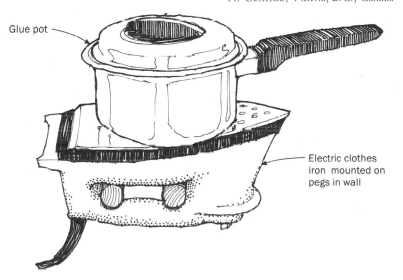

Glue pot

Electric clothes iron mounted on pegs in wall

Repairing Cracks

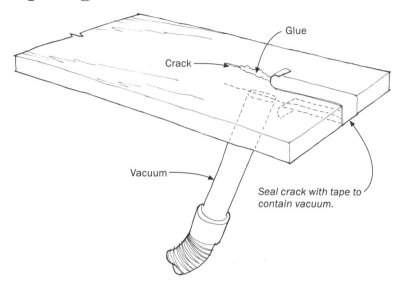

Glue

Crack

Vacuum

Seal crack with tape to contain vacuum.

I N THE PROCESS OF repairing furniture or using seasoned lumber, we occasionally encounter a split board. Depending on the severity of the crack and the value of the lumber, it is sometimes desirable to repair the crack. A vacuum cleaner, masking tape, clamps, and glue can accomplish this. Tape over the crack, down the end of the board, and on the underside of the crack. The object is to create a vacuum.

With a crevice tool on the vacuum cleaner, suck the glue into the crack while slowly peeling back the masking tape. Add glue while sliding the crevice tool out to the end of the board. Once the crack is filled with glue, clamp the split closed. The viscosity of glue is usually sufficient to prevent it from being sucked into the vacuum-cleaner hose. To be safe, remove the hose as soon as glue is visible on the underside. A little experimentation will show you how much time, glue, and tape to use.

—RAY SCHWENN, *Jamesville, N.Y.*

Tape Measure Glue-Insertion Tool

I'M SURE MOST WOODWORKERS have been faced with the problem of trying to force glue into a tight split or crack in the workpiece. My solution for this problem is to cut a 6-in. or so section from an old tape measure. Then I cut a profile on the end of the tape, varying the shape for different applications. The tape section is thin but stiff, and it's ideal for working glue into a crevice.

—GREGORY H. JOY, *Lincoln, Nebr.*

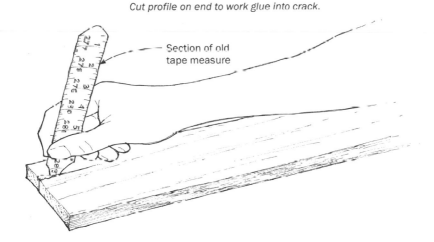

Cut profile on end to work glue into crack.

Section of old tape measure

Metal Pins Eliminate Miter Slippage

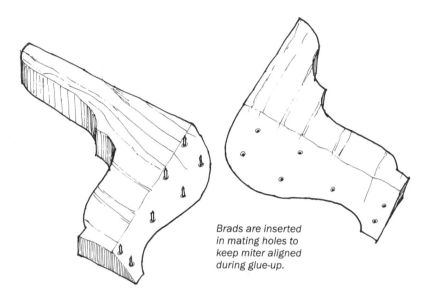

Brads are inserted in mating holes to keep miter aligned during glue-up.

T HIS METHOD OF USING metal pins to prevent miter slippage during glue-up is good on odd-shaped mitered pieces, like the bracket feet in the sketch, that might otherwise require special clamping jigs.

Start by placing one of the joint halves, miter side up, on the drill-press table. Select a bit the same size as an 18-gauge brad, and begin drilling shallow holes in the miter face in a pattern that suits the job. Place brads in these holes, nip the heads off flush with a side cutter, and then fish each brad out of its hole and reverse it end for end so the point is up. Now align the two halves of the mitered molding, and push straight down on the sharp pin points. The mating half will have an exact layout for drilling a matching set of pin holes.

After the holes have been drilled in the mating half, remove the original pins. Put new brads in the original holes, cut these to a suitable length, and reverse them to put the points up. I find it helpful to countersink each of the holes slightly, to help each pin "find" its matching hole and ensure the assembly goes smoothly.

The joint can now be put together dry and pressed tight. If you have been careful, the joint will fit almost perfectly. A slight overlap can usually be corrected by a small amount of pressure or twisting.

—J. A. BINNS, *Tucson, Ariz.*

Uses for Tongue Depressors

TONGUE DEPRESSORS ARE HANDY for spreading glue, stirring paint, padding clamps, shimming, and so on. They're available at drugstores in boxes of 750 for less than a penny each.

—STANLEY BESSENT, *Goldthwaite, Tex.*

Catching Glue Squeeze-Out with Tape

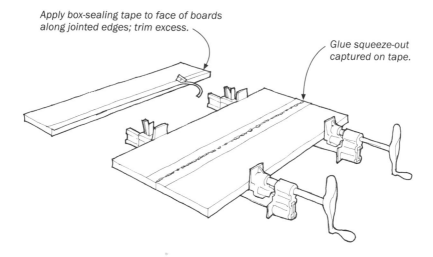

Apply box-sealing tape to face of boards
along jointed edges; trim excess.

Glue squeeze-out
captured on tape.

HERE'S A TECHNIQUE THAT keeps squeeze-out off the wood when
you're gluing up panels. When the boards have been jointed,
just before gluing, apply a strip of box-sealing tape on the face of each
board along the jointed edge. Let the tape overhang the jointed edges
by ¼ in. or so. Press the tape tightly along the corners. Then trim the
overhang with a new safety razor, taking care not to nick the jointed
edges. Glue as usual. Any glue squeeze-out will go onto the face of
the tape and not onto your panel.

After the glue cures, remove the clamps, and pull the two pieces of
tape off the joint. There may be a hairline bead of glue at the seam,
but this is easily removed. Don't let the tape stay on the work too long
because the adhesive may become hard to remove.

The best tape for this job is 3M's Scotch premium commercial
box-sealing tape. Avoid using duct tape, masking tape, cheap packing
tape, or regular Scotch tape.

I much prefer spending the time applying tape than scraping glue residue, which can cause finishing problems. Taping also has the advantage of isolating clamp bars from the stock, thus eliminating iron stains.

—JIM WRIGHT, *Berkley, Mass.*

Removing Excess Glue with Sawdust

T O REMOVE EXCESS GLUE squeezed out of a clamped joint, first scoop up the bulk of the glue with one of the loose subscription cards found in each issue of *Fine Woodworking*. Next, grab a handful of sawdust, preferably from the wood being glued, and rub it around, which will create little balls of glue and sawdust that will remove all traces of the glue.

—PHIL HALL, *N. Berwick, Maine*

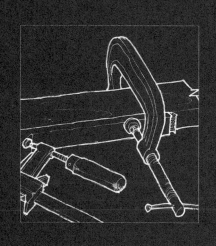

Chapter 9

CLAMPING

Improvised Edge Clamp

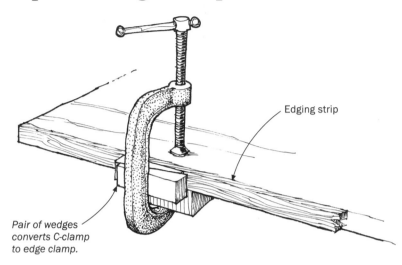

Edging strip

Pair of wedges
converts C-clamp
to edge clamp.

T O IMPROVISE AN EDGE clamp, all you need is a regular C-clamp and a couple of wedges. If the clamp's back is curved where it hits the wedges, use a block to realign the back to a straight section.

—DON H. ANDERSON, *Sequim, Wash.*

Modified C-Clamps

ALMOST ALL C-CLAMPS have sliding bars through the end of the screw for tightening. But when you have to use several clamps close together, as you do when gluing laminations to a curved form, for example, these bars get in the way. On a recent project, I finally got annoyed with the interfering handles, so I removed the tightening bars and welded nuts to the ends of the clamp's screws. Now I can easily take up the slack by twisting the screws with my thumb and forefinger and then give each a final tightening with a short-handled socket wrench. As an added bonus, the clamps stack up neatly on a storage post.

—JACK JEROME, *Nokomis, Fla.*

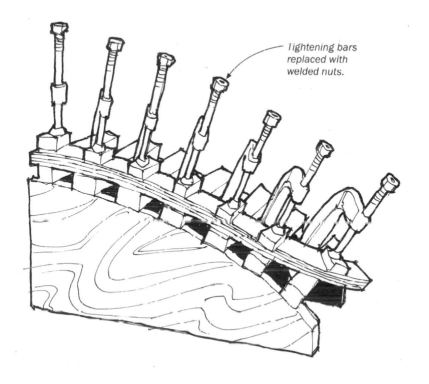

Tightening bars replaced with welded nuts.

Wedges for Edging Plywood

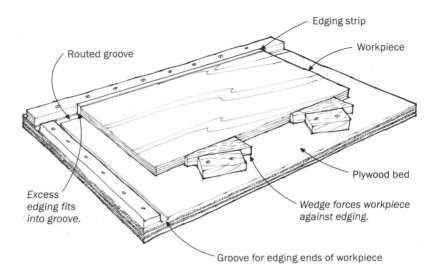

Edging strip

Routed groove

Workpiece

Plywood bed

Excess
edging fits
into groove.

Wedge forces workpiece
against edging.

Groove for edging ends of workpiece

H ERE IS A METHOD that I use to attach ⅜-in.-thick, solid-wood
edging to ¾-in.-thick plywood shelves and case members.

To make my edge-gluing fixture, as shown in the sketch, cut a
panel of inexpensive ¾-in.-thick fir plywood to serve as the bed. In
this bed, rout a ⅜-in.-wide by ¹⁄₁₆-in.-deep groove about 1½ in. from
the edge. Screw a batten along the edge of the plywood so that the
batten slightly overhangs the routed groove. Now, saw several wedges,
all the same size and taper, and an equal number of rectangular pressure blocks about 1 in. shorter than the wedges. With a simple workpiece in place in the jig, screw the blocks to the bed, as shown, so that
the wedges can be tapped home.

To use the jig for ¾-in.-thick shelves, first rip ⅜-in.-wide solid-wood edging from a board that has been planed to ⅞ in. thick. Cut the edging to length, and place it in the groove against the batten. Spread glue along the edge of the workpiece, lay it against the edging, and tap the wedges home with a hammer.

After the glue has set, tap the narrow end of each wedge to unclamp the work, and remove the workpiece from the jig. Trim the edging flush with the plywood surface using a router jig or hand-plane. To edgeband the ends of the workpieces, follow the same procedure but with the groove and batten located at the end of the plywood bed.

—ABRAM LOFT, *Rochester, N.Y.*

Using Quick-Grip Bar Clamps As Hold-Downs

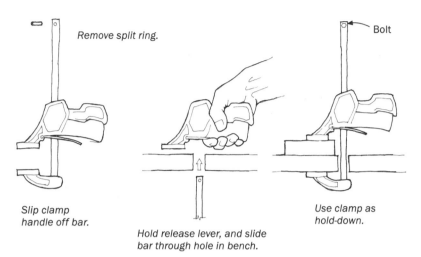

Remove split ring.

Bolt

Slip clamp handle off bar.

Hold release lever, and slide bar through hole in bench.

Use clamp as hold-down.

HERE'S HOW TO USE A Quick-Grip bar clamp as a hold-down: Locate the bench-dog hole where you want to position the hold-down, or drill a ¾-in. hole through the benchtop. Now punch out the split ring on the end of the bar, hold down the release lever of the pistol grip, and slide the grip assembly off the bar. Don't let go of the release lever, or you will have to realign the retention washers and spring inside the grip. Guide the bar through the hole in the bench, and slide the grip assembly back onto the bar. Replace the split ring with a ¼-in. bolt and wing nut to facilitate future changeovers.

—MATT VALIKOSKI, *Campbell River, B.C., Canada*

Spring Clips for Clamping

WHEN MAKING BENTWOOD LAMINATIONS, I never had enough clamps until I began using spring clips available at the stationery store. The clips come in several sizes and are cheap, lightweight, and strong.

—STEVE BORTON, *Vancouver, B.C., Canada*

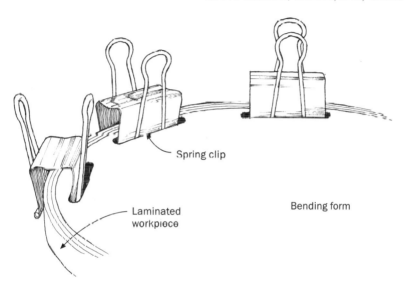

Spring clip

Laminated
workpiece

Bending form

Long-Reach Clamping

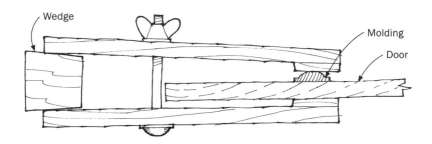

M OST C-CLAMPS DO NOT have very long reaches, and special long-reach clamps are too expensive to have around for just occasional use. So, when I needed to glue molding on the flat face of a door, about 5 in. from the edge, I adapted a system I used in my boat-building days.

In boat work, when parts had to be held together far from an edge, we fastened two boards loosely together with a nut and bolt. Then, we adjusted the bolt so that when a wedge was driven between the open ends, the other ends would clamp down on the parts.

For my door-molding application, driving a wedge into the clamping strips would have moved the molding. So I carefully placed the wedge in position without hammering and then simply tightened the clamp arms with a wing nut.

—PERCY BLANDFORD, *Stratford-upon-Avon, England*

Go-Bars for Clamping

I FIRST LEARNED ABOUT GO-BARS during a visit to the shop of William Dowd, a harpsichord builder. A go-bar is simply a thin strip of wood flexed by hand into a bow shape and inserted between a fixed surface, such as a ceiling, and the surface of a workpiece to be clamped. Harpsichord makers use go-bars for gluing the soundboard of their instrument into the carcase because no ordinary kind of clamp can be brought easily to bear on the work. But go-bars can be applied to a much broader range of clamping problems. They are not only simpler and less expensive than other clamps but also much easier and faster to set.

To make go-bars, start with straight-grain wood. I've used ¾-in.-thick fir flooring sawn into ½-in.-wide strips for 39 in. long go-bars. Experiment with your own wood-and-clamping conditions to get the dimensions right. Cut the bars about 2 or 3 percent longer than the distance between the work surface and the fixed surface. This will cause the bars to bow out about a fifth of their length, which should feel about right.

—ABIJAH REED, *Newton Centre, Mass.*

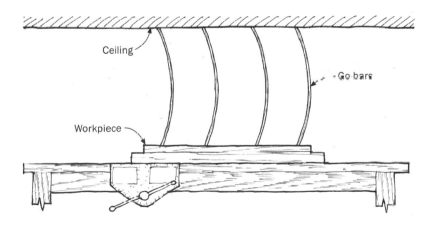

Ceiling Joist Clamping

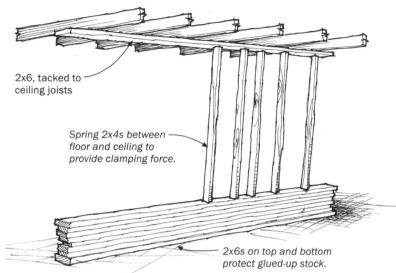

2x6, tacked to ceiling joists

Spring 2x4s between floor and ceiling to provide clamping force.

2x6s on top and bottom protect glued-up stock.

HERE'S A QUICK AND EASY technique that I use to laminate 2x4s into larger beams. First, lay a 2x6 on the floor, and level it to a 2x6 tacked to your shop ceiling. Make sure that the 2x6 on the ceiling runs at a right angle to the ceiling joists. Now, one by one, quickly roll glue on the face of each 2x4 and stack the laminates. Cover the stack with another 2x6, and then spring precut 2x4s between the stack and ceiling to provide clamping pressure. The large amount of force is surprising; be careful you don't lift the joists too far.

—DAVID FOOS, *Los Angeles, Calif.*

Car-Jack Veneer Press

THIS VENEER PRESS IS EASILY made with a scissors–type auto jack and any available lumber. Hinge the arm of the press to a plate that you've attached to the shop ceiling joists. Use a sleeve in the arm to allow different-length lower posts to be inserted, depending on the veneering job at hand.

—HECTOR MACLEAN, *Weston, Ont., Canada*

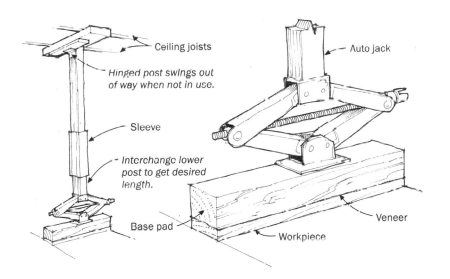

Ceiling joists

Hinged post swings out of way when not in use.

Auto jack

Sleeve

Interchange lower post to get desired length.

Base pad

Workpiece

Veneer

Car-Jack Bar Clamps

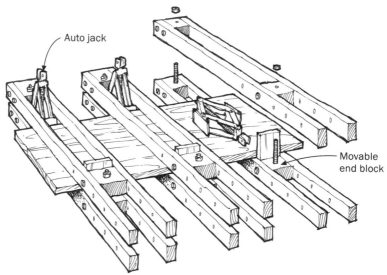

Auto jack

Movable
end block

Here's a way to make low-tech wooden bar clamps for gluing up panels, tabletops, and the like. The inexpensive clamps, which utilize salvaged scissors-style auto jacks for the main component, adjust to any thickness of stock and automatically align the stock being glued. Also, the parts are bolted instead of glued together, so you can easily replace any damaged component.

To build the clamps, select 1-in. or thicker dense hardwood, and make the various parts as shown in the sketch above. To use the clamps, first bolt the moveable end blocks into the appropriate hole that correlates to the size panel you're gluing up. Then place the work on the lower tier of clamps and apply glue to the edges. Next, slide on the upper parts of the clamps and hand-tighten the nuts to align the boards being glued up. Last of all, insert and tighten the car jacks to put edge pressure on the glued lumber.

—Koji Katsuragi, *Kumamoto, Japan*

Clamping Wide Boards

IN BOOKCASE CONSTRUCTION AND other large-carcase work, it is often necessary to join wide boards in an H. Without special clamps, it is difficult to achieve the necessary clamping pressure. This simple crowned caul, used with ordinary bar clamps, solves the problem.

To make the caul, select a 1-in.-thick, 2-in.-wide block as long as your lumber is wide. Plane a crown on one edge, leaving the center high and each end about a degree lower. Now lay the caul, crown edge down, across the width of the board to be clamped. As you apply pressure to each end with bar clamps, the end-gaps will close, resulting in even pressure across the joint.

—DAVID SHAFFER, *Silvercliff, Colo.*

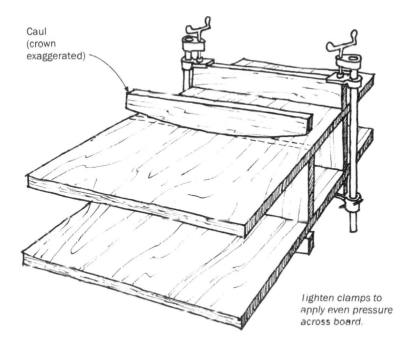

Caul
(crown
exaggerated)

Tighten clamps to
apply even pressure
across board.

Adjustable Shopmade Clamps

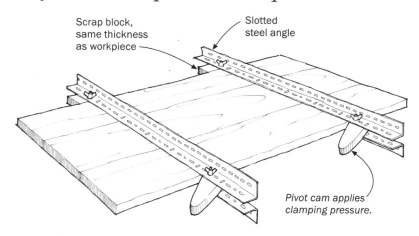

Scrap block, same thickness as workpiece

Slotted steel angle

Pivot cam applies clamping pressure.

WOODWORKERS NEEDING TO edge-join boards on a regular basis should consider using slotted-steel angles to construct a clamping jig. The slotted angle is available in a variety of weights and strengths for use in shelving systems in libraries and warehouses. Holes or slots are punched along the length of the material for a variety of bolt placements.

A clamping jig can be made by fixing two pieces of the angle together with bolts and wing nuts at each end. One bolt secures a fixed spacer the same thickness as the planks to be edge-glued. The other bolt holds a cam clamp, also of the same thickness, which applies pressure to the plank edges when the whole clamp is assembled.

—A. W. CLARKE, *Moonta Mines, Australia*

Making Clamps

FOR MANY PEOPLE WHO aren't professional cabinetmakers, wooden clamps are in the luxury-tool class. Good commercially-made handscrews cost at least $15 in the 8-in. size. Materials to make one cost less than $5.

Make the jaws from maple or another dense hardwood. The ½-in. holes must be carefully drilled square to the jaw surface and the same distance apart. The spindles are ⁵⁄₁₆-in. steel bar. All threads are ⁵⁄₁₆-18. Thread 5-in. of one end of the spindles right handed and 3-in. of the opposite ends left handed. Make the nuts from ½-in. round bar. Be sure the tapped holes are square to the axis of the bar. Small file handles will work well if you don't have a lathe. Drill through the ferrule and spindle and insert a small pin after assembly.

RICHARD E. PRICE, *Seattle, Wa.*

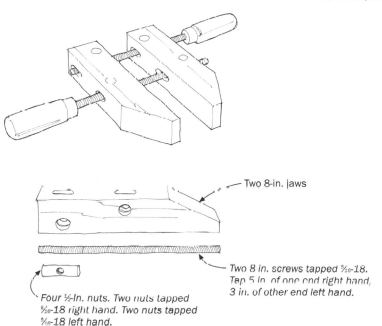

— Two 8-in. jaws

— Two 8 in. screws tapped ⁵⁄₁₆-18.
Tap 5 in. of one end right hand,
3 in. of other end left hand.

Four ½-In. nuts. Two nuts tapped
⁵⁄₁₆-18 right hand. Two nuts tapped
⁵⁄₁₆-18 left hand.

Double-Duty Edge-Gluing Clamps

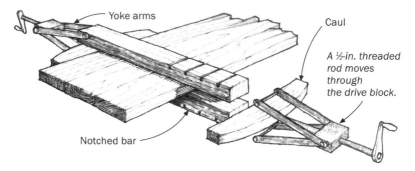

Yoke arms

Caul

A ½-in. threaded rod moves through the drive block.

Notched bar

T HIS SHOP–BUILT EDGE–GLUING clamp performs double duty. It is not only a terrific bar clamp, but it also aligns the various work-pieces being glued, thus eliminating the need for a separate alignment "sandwich" made with scrap and C-clamps.

The clamps consist of two yokes and two notched wooden bars. Each yoke assembly has a pair of trapeze-like arms made from 8-in.-long pieces of strap iron that pivot on the sides of a block made from ¾-in.-thick mild steel. Drill and tap a hole through the block to accept a ½-in. threaded drive rod. Then, drill and tap ¼-in. holes in the sides of the block to bolt the arms in place.

Next, screw a length of ½-in. threaded rod through the block and attach a knob or crank to its outboard end. To distribute clamping pressure, make a wooden caul with a shallow ½-in. hole bored in its edge to locate the end of the rod. Plane a shallow concave curve in the caul edge that contacts the work to ensure even distribution of clamping pressure.

Cut the clamp's notched wooden bars from 1¼-in.-thick sticks of hardwood. The bars should be as wide as the space in the yoke arms. To make sure the notches in the bars are perfectly aligned, cut both bars at the same time with a ¼-in. dado blade.

—WILLIAM SWARTZ, *Modesto, Calif.*

Homemade Edge-Gluing Clamps

H ERE'S AN INEXPENSIVE BUT effective homemade clamp for edge-gluing stock. Unlike a pipe clamp, it won't fall off the work-piece while you're fitting up and it pulls evenly on both sides of the stock, ensuring flat panels. To use, pin the sliding tail block in an appropriate place, then apply pressure by screwing down a C-clamp across the wedges. Scraps of waxed paper will shield the clamp from glue squeeze-out.

—BERT WHITCHURCH, *Rockaway Beach, Mo.*

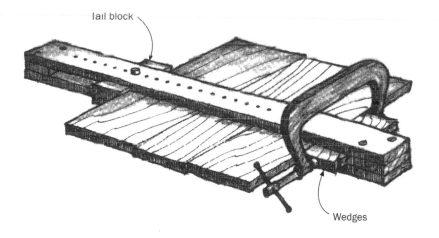

Tail block

Wedges

Toolmaker's Clamp

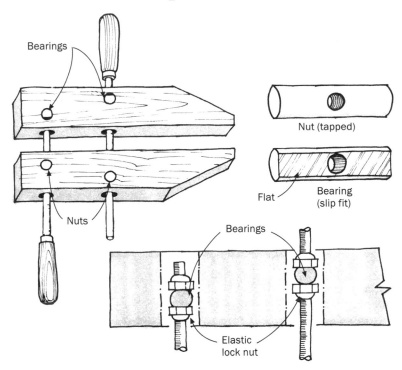

I 'VE SEEN SEVERAL WOODEN clamp designs presented in "Methods of Work" in *Fine Woodworking* but none similar to what machinists know as a toolmaker's clamp. It is constructed like a standard wooden clamp but uses fixed bearing surfaces in place of the left-handed threaded rods and barrel-nuts. Because the toolmaker's clamp uses standard hardware-store threaded rod, it is much easier to build. Only a right-hand tap and drill bits are needed to complete the metal work.

Although the barrel-nuts can be made from either brass or steel, make the bearings out of brass (steel would soon gall the thrust surfaces). File a flat on each of the two bearings and turn the flat toward the side that takes the thrust. The thrust-nuts that bear up against the bearings must be locked into position on the threaded rod. I have found that elastic lock-nuts work well, but a pair of jam-nuts or a single nut brazed to the threaded rod could be substituted.

Both barrel-nuts must be located in one jaw and both bearings in the other jaw to get the standard tightening and loosening rotation. It will take twice as many turns to close the toolmaker's clamp, but you get twice the clamping force for the same tightening torque.

—LARRY PAGENDARM, *Santa Clara, Calif.*

Simple Hand Clamp

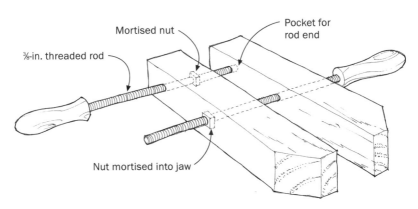

Mortised nut

Pocket for rod end

⅜-in. threaded rod

Nut mortised into jaw

H ERE IS A SIMPLE HAND clamp that can be made without any threading or tapping—the only tools needed are a drill and a chisel. The idea is taken from old wooden handscrews that were given to me a few years back. There are no reverse threads and the jaws open and close parallel to each other. I hold the center handle in my left hand and spin the clamp around it clockwise to close the jaws; this keeps the jaws parallel until they are the desired distance apart. A turn or so on the rear handle then supplies enough pressure for any glue joint.

The threaded parts are ⅜-in. threaded rod sold at hardware stores. Get nuts to match and simply mortise them into the hardwood jaws. If the mortises are loose, you can use epoxy glue to hold the nuts in place; use just a dab and keep it away from the threads. The holes are drilled ½ in. to allow easy passage of the rod. The turned handles are held firmly on the rod with epoxy glue pushed into a slightly oversize and overdeep hole.

—ALBERT C. LANDRY, *Richmond, Maine*

Clothespin Clamps

I MAKE HEAVY-DUTY CLOTHESPIN clamps from two hardwood sticks (½ in. square by 7 in. long), a short ⅜-in. dowel fulcrum, and a heavy rubber band (about ¼ in. by 4 in. long). The dowel fulcrum fits in slight hollows filed in the sticks about one-third the way from the front. Dull the sharp edges of the sticks, then double the rubber band around the two sides in front of the fulcrum as many times as possible.

I use this clamp for gluing the linings onto the sides of musical instruments. But by making a few changes the same basic clamp can be used for other applications. For example, different jaw capacities or parallel-jaw clamping can be achieved by using different-sized fulcrums. The weight of the rubber band can be varied for more or less clamping pressure. The jaws can be notched to clamp unusually shaped work.

I also have some commercial steel-spring clamps, but my home-made clothespins clamp with more pressure.

—BART BRUSH, *Cherry Valley, N.Y.*

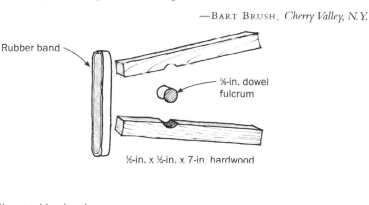

Rubber band

⅜-in. dowel fulcrum

½-in. x ½-in. x 7-in. hardwood

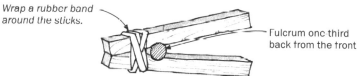

Wrap a rubber band around the sticks.

Fulcrum one-third back from the front

Homemade Bar Clamps

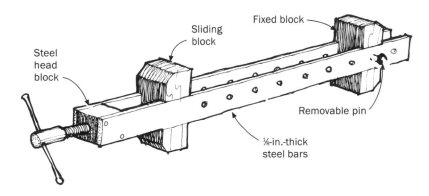

OU CAN NEVER BE TOO thin, too rich, or have too many bar
clamps. But a woodworker's cash usually goes toward tools and
machinery, leaving clamps for another day. The homemade model
above, though made from light, cheap material, will do most (though
not all) things a bar clamp will do.

The two bars are made of mild steel, ¾ in. wide by ⅛ in. thick.
Clamp the two bars together and drill ¼-in. holes spaced 1½ in. apart.
Make the head block from a ¾-in. cube of steel tapped for a ⅜-in.
threaded rod. With the head block carefully lined up and clamped in
position, fasten it to the bars by welding, brazing, or riveting.

Make the 2¼-in. by 1-in. by 1-in. sliding block and the fixed block
from any dense hardwood. Cut a ⅛-in.-deep groove on each side of
the blocks to give a sliding fit between the bars. Drill a shallow ⅜-in.
hole in the sliding block to take the end of the threaded rod. So the
rod won't continually bore its way into the wood, force a pellet of
⅜-in. steel into the bottom of the hole.

Braze a short length of pipe onto the end of the threaded rod and drill it to accept a tommy bar of ¼-in. steel rod. Peen the ends of the tommy bar to keep it from falling out of the hole. In use, the work is slid between the bars to ensure even clamping pressure, and the fixed block is moved and pinned in the appropriate place for the width of the work.

This clamp will handle work up to ¾ in. thick and perhaps 24 in. wide. The clamp could be scaled up using heavier materials for thicker or wider applications.

An alternative use for the clamp is to prevent "spelching" (the splitting off of the end grain during handplaning). Move the clamp to the edge of the board so its blocks are flush with the end grain. The clamp may be used many times before its wood blocks need replacing.

—ROBERT WEARING, *Shropshire, England*

Turnbuckle Clamp

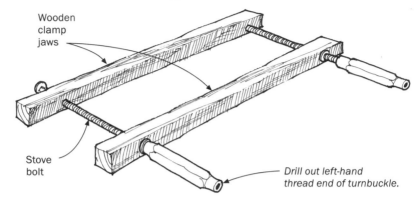

Wooden clamp jaws

Stove bolt

Drill out left-hand thread end of turnbuckle.

I MAKE AN INEXPENSIVE BOX clamp from turnbuckles, long stove bolts, washers, and scrapwood. Remove the ring bolts from the turnbuckles and drill out the threads on one end.

—DAN WILSON, *Chesterfield, Mo.*

Magnetic Pipe-Clamp Pads

THE BEST PIPE-CLAMP PADS I've seen were made by facing hardboard with sticky-back magnetic tape. The hardboard is hard enough to resist deforming, yet soft enough to not mark softer woods like walnut and mahogany. The magnetic tape holds the pads in place better than a third hand, and the pads are easily removed. Magnetic tape (I used 3M Plastiform brand) can be obtained locally at sign shops and some hardware stores, or it can be mail-ordered from Woodcraft, 560 Airport Industrial Park, Parkersburg, WV 26102-1686.

—MIKE GRAETZ, *Lakeland, Minn.*

Clamping Pads for Bar Clamps

I DON'T HAVE A THIRD hand to hold a non-marring pad under the
screw of my bar clamp. So I cut a slot in a scrap piece of Masonite
and attached it loosely to the clamp bar with a rubber band. To pad
the other end, I glued a piece of shoe leather to the clamp jaw.

—TED TEDESCHI, *Prescott Valley, Ariz.*

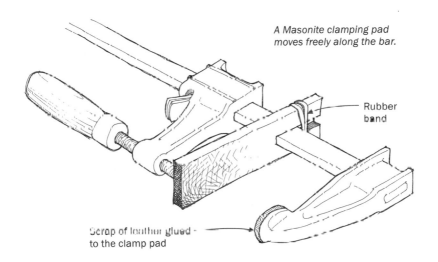

A Masonite clamping pad
moves freely along the bar.

Rubber
band

Scrap of leather glued
to the clamp pad

Bar-Clamp Stain Protectors

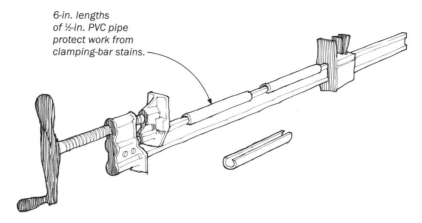

6-in. lengths of ½-in. PVC pipe protect work from clamping-bar stains.

I N THE PROCESS OF collecting materials to glue up a tabletop, I discovered that I was out of waxed paper. I always used waxed paper between my work and the bar clamps to prevent the black stains that invariably result when aliphatic-resin glue, iron, and wood combine for any length of time.

In looking around for a suitable alternative, I remembered a short length of ½-in. schedule 40 PVC pipe I had. I cut the pipe lengthwise with my bandsaw to reveal a slot just under ½ in. Then I cut the pipe into convenient 6-in. segments and snapped the segments over the iron bars of the clamps. If the slot is the right width, the segments will grip the bars and stay in place even when the clamps are turned over or hung up to store.

—THORNTON TRAISE, *Omaha, Neb.*

Reversing Pipe Clamps

I T's HANDY TO BE able to reverse a pipe clamp so it can be used to push something apart. In fact, special clamp heads are sold for this purpose. As a thrifty alternative, if you add a short section of pipe to the head as shown below, you'll be able to reverse any standard pipe clamp at will.

Screw the head on backwards and stop about halfway. Then screw the short 6-in. piece into the clamp head in the normal fashion. Reverse the shoe, and you have an efficient spreading clamp.

—T.D. CULVER, *Cleveland Heights, Ohio*

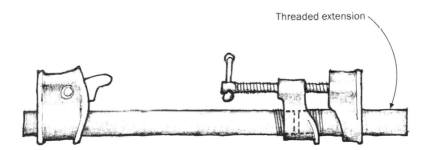

Threaded extension

Furniture Disassembly Jack

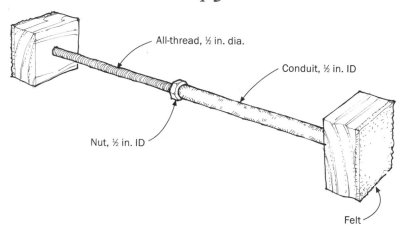

All-thread, ½ in. dia.

Conduit, ½ in. ID

Nut, ½ in. ID

Felt

THOSE OF US WHO Repair furniture often come across a chair or table that is so loose it needs to be totally disassembled and reglued. But invariably there are always two or three joints that, unlike the rest of the rickety piece, will not come apart no matter what. I use a shopmade jack to solve this problem. The jack, shown in the sketch above, is composed of a short length of ½-in. conduit, a piece of ½-in.-dia. all-thread, a nut, and two padded blocks. When you tighten the nut against the end of the conduit, even the most reluctant joint will give up, usually with no damage.

—LEE CROWDER, *Easton, Md.*

Picture-Frame Clamp

THIS PICTURE-FRAME CLAMP beats anything else I've tried. Make the device from ¾-in.-thick, 2-in.-wide hardwood strips. I covered the hardwood with smooth Formica for extra strength and for freer action of the parts. You'll need four 16-in. legs, two 4-in. connectors, and four 2-in. discs notched to hold the corners of the frame.

To use, determine the positions of the notched discs on the legs through a dry run. When everything is ready, apply pressure to the frame using a parallel-jaw wooden clamp across the center connectors.

—JOHN L. VAN SCOYOC, *Bartlesville, Okla.*

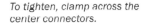

To tighten, clamp across the center connectors.

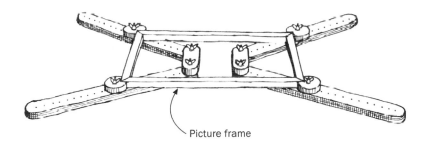

Picture frame

Low-Cost Picture-Frame Clamp

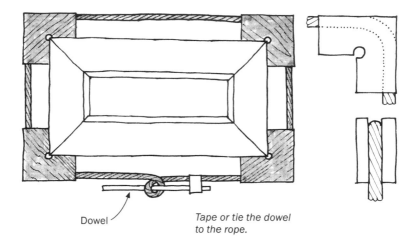

Dowel

Tape or tie the dowel
to the rope.

MY PICTURE-FRAME CLAMP uses a tourniquet to apply pressure
at the glue joints. To make the clamp, cut four L-shaped
clamping blocks from ¾-in. pine and groove the outside edges of the
blocks a little wider than the rope diameter. Then round, smooth, and
wax the grooves to minimize friction. Cut or drill a circular area at
the inside corner of the blocks to allow for slight inaccuracies (which
accumulate at that point) and to permit excess glue to escape. When
you're ready to glue, place a piece of waxed paper under each block to
prevent it from becoming glued to the frame.

For the rope, choose something with a little stretch—I use ⅛-in. nylon. Tie a loop in the rope just long enough so that it can barely be snapped over the blocks. This will hold the frame together while final adjustments are made in the glue joints. When the joints are right, twist a dowel onto the rope and turn it to produce whatever pressure is desired. The leverage is tremendous so don't overdo it. It's a good idea to put a weight on the frame while you're applying pressure. If one corner comes up a little, the whole assembly may twist and fly apart.

When the pressure is sufficient, tape or tie the dowel to the rope. Always maintain a tight grip on the dowel—it can unwind with surprising force.

—H. N. CAPEN, *Granada Hills, Calif.*

Clamping Picture Frames with Coil Springs

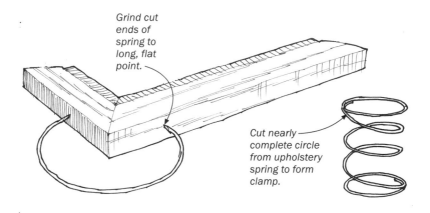

Grind cut ends of spring to long, flat point.

Cut nearly complete circle from upholstery spring to form clamp.

HERE'S A METHOD OF CLAMPING picture frames that I learned years ago at the shop of a New York City framemaker. Use spring clamps made from upholsterer's coil springs to exert pressure. The sharpened ends of the circular springs bite into the sides of the mitered frame pieces, putting pressure exactly where it's needed—on the glued miter.

To make the rings, saw nearly complete circles from the coil springs. Then carefully sharpen the cut ends on a belt sander or grinding wheel to form long, flat points. Two upholsterer's coil springs will yield two or three complete sets of four spring clamps of various sizes and tensions.

—STEVE MANVILLE, *Amagansett, N.Y.*

Miter Clamping Blocks

THESE AUXILIARY CLAMPING BLOCKS provide an easy and inexpensive way to clamp mitered workpieces. Bandsaw the blocks from a piece of hardwood scrap the same thickness as the stock being glued. For 90° corners, angle the face of the clamping block at 45°. For other odd angles, cut the face at half the angle of the finished joint.

To use, secure a clamping block to each side of the miter joint with a C-clamp. Add a strip of double-faced sandpaper between the clamp block and the workpiece. I make the sandpaper strips by gluing 180-grit sandpaper back to back. The sandpaper layer eliminates slippage with no harm to the workpiece. Spread glue on the joint surfaces, and clamp across the joint with a quick-acting bar clamp.

—ILMARS VILMANIS, *St. Petersburg, Fla.*

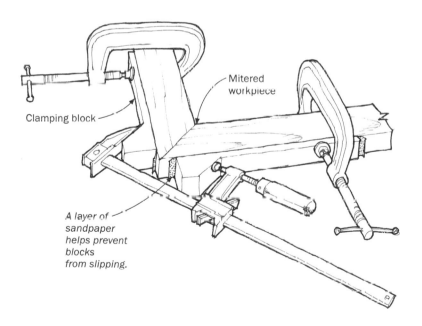

Mitered workpiece

Clamping block

A layer of sandpaper helps prevent blocks from slipping.

Spur Dogs for Clamping Miters

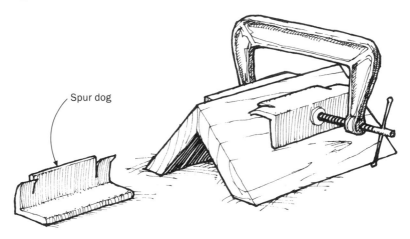

Spur dog

H ERE IS A METHOD that allows you to clamp up mitered edges. The method is based on a spur dog, a device that provides a perch for C-clamps and spreads clamping pressure evenly over the joint. To make the dogs, cut several pairs of 3-in. sections from a length of 1-in. angle iron. In each section, hacksaw two ⁵⁄₁₆-in.-deep slots about ½ in. from each end of one side. Bend the two tabs down about ³⁄₃₂ in. and file the spurs sharp, as shown in the sketch above.

To use, spread glue on both faces of the miter and press together for a light tack. Tap the two (or more) dogs into place and clamp. The spurs enter the wood grain about ⅛ in. and therefore leave small scars on the wood. These scars can be removed by rounding over the corner, or they can be closed up some by steaming. You might decide to simply tolerate them.

—PETER BIRD, *Midhurst, Ont., Canada*

Edge-Gluing Setup
Handles Angled Boards

A FTER MANY TRIALS AND some wasted materials, I finally discovered this effective technique for clamping boards that are at a slight angle. Dry-run the clamping until the stops are located perfectly. I'd recommend using a slow-setting glue such as Franklin hide glue. If needed, clamp the central area of the boards by running a caul across them with a clamp on each side.

—W. G. SHEARD, *Horseheads, N.Y.*

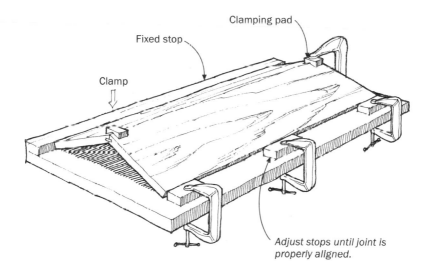

Clamping pad

Fixed stop

Clamp

Adjust stops until joint is properly aligned.

Clamping Splined Miters

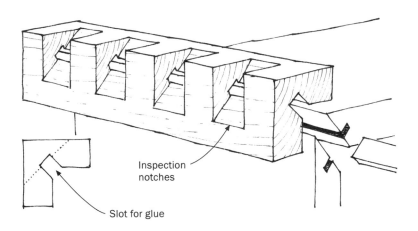

Inspection notches

Slot for glue

H ERE'S AN IMPROVED CLAMPING block for spline-miter joints. My set has been used to make at least a hundred joints.

The glue block is basically an L-profile block with two additions— a channel cut in the inside corner to allow for exuded glue and a series of inspection slots cut into the outside corner of the block to see if the joint is pulled together evenly. The blocks can be used with strap or bar clamps.

—R. H. NORTON, *Shalimar, Fla.*

Modifying Handscrews
to Clamp Mitered Frames

TO CLAMP MITERED FRAMES, you can squeeze the joint via pocket holes drilled in the back of the adjacent parts. Two manufacturers offer clamps for this: Universal Edge-to-Edge clamp (W. MacNiven Conard, P.O. Box 250, Vershire, VT 05079; 802-685-4441) and Jorgensen adapter tips (Adjustable Clamp Co., 417 N. Ashland Ave., Chicago, IL 60622; 312-666-0640).

To make your own clamps, add metal pins to a handscrew, as shown below. Make the pins by screwing bolts into tapped holes and then cutting or grinding off the heads. To use, drill holes in the back of the frame, and use the pins to apply pressure. Angle the tips toward the center of the work.

—GLEN CARLSON, *San Diego, Calif.*

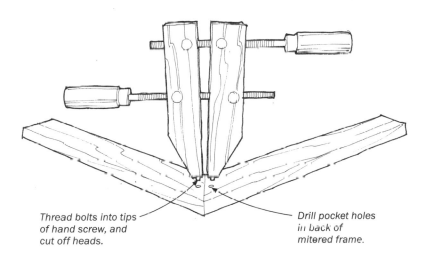

Thread bolts into tips
of hand screw, and
cut off heads.

Drill pocket holes
in back of
mitered frame.

Clamping Aid for Odd Angles

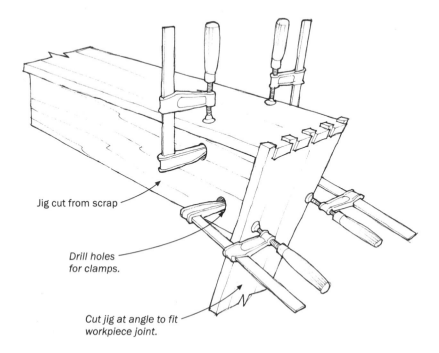

Jig cut from scrap

Drill holes
for clamps.

Cut jig at angle to fit
workpiece joint.

I T IS FRUSTRATING TO clamp together two boards precisely at an
odd-angled corner. This jig, which can be made quickly from scrap
lumber, will help. Cut a generous scrap of hardwood to the appropriate corner angle, and drill holes through the scrap, as shown above, to
accommodate the head of a clamp. Use two clamps for each jig piece,
one on each of the two boards forming the corner. Make sure the
inside corner of the joint is firm against the jig. One jig should suffice
for joining narrow boards. Wider pieces will need two jigs, one on
each edge, as shown.

—KEITH R. ALLEN, *Cedar Grove, N.C.*

Rubber Band Clamps

A WOODWORKING FRIEND OF MINE once grumbled that he wished he were in Heaven because "In Heaven they have enough clamps." This common lament came back to me recently as I attempted to glue edging strips to plywood shelves with too few clamps. So I decided to try to make some clamps using rubber bands and hooks.

A trip to the stationery store revealed that rubber bands come in many different sizes and styles. I bought a box of the largest they had, which were about ⅛ in. wide and 7 in. long. A trip to the hardware store yielded a supply of ¾-in., open S-hooks. I attached a hook to each rubber band by bending the hook closed using a pair of pliers. The other end of the hook stays open to clasp the other end of the same rubber band.

—JOHN B. MOON, *Mount Vernon, Wash.*

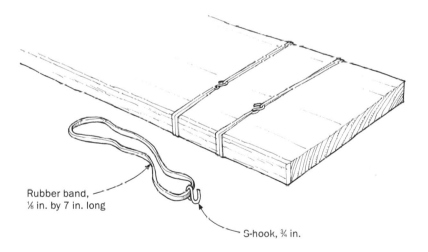

Rubber band,
⅛ in. by 7 in. long

S-hook, ¾ in.

Light-Duty Band Clamp

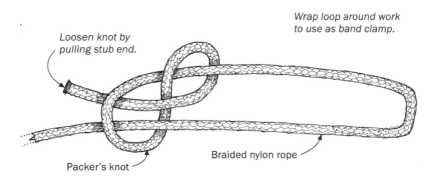

Loosen knot by pulling stub end.

Wrap loop around work to use as band clamp.

Packer's knot

Braided nylon rope

A BAND CLAMP IS INDISPENSABLE for assembling mitered boxes, picture frames, chair frames, and the like. All you need to make a light-duty band clamp is a length of ⁹⁄₁₆-in.-dia. braided nylon rope tied in a packer's knot. The rope is available at most hardware stores and is cheap, strong, easy to store, and won't mar the wood. The knot, illustrated above in case you've misplaced your trusty Boy Scout Handbook, will hold all the pressure you can put on it but will loosen easily when you jerk the stub end.

Since discovering this band clamp, I've stopped using looped rubber bands and strips of inner tube because they are more difficult to apply and store.

—ROBERT VAUGHAN, *Roanoke, Va.*

Rubber-Strip Clamp

ONE OF THE MOST VERSATILE clamps in my shop is a 1-in.-wide strip of rubber from an old inner tube that I cut in a continuous spiral. I've used the clamp for some of my trickiest jobs, like edging plywood, clamping picture frames, regluing chair legs, and repairing a gusset brace on an antique chair. The strip is also handy as a supplement to conventional clamps on some jobs. But versatility is not the clamp's only advantage; it costs nothing and will never mar the wood.

—BERNARD PEARSON, *Mississauga, Ont., Canada*

Cut a strip from an inner tube in a continuous spiral.

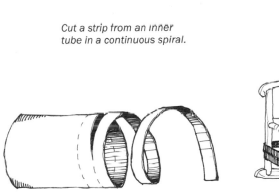

Spanish Luthier's Clamp

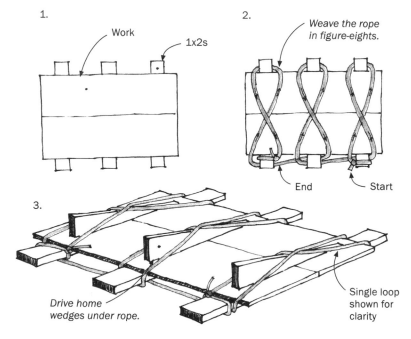

1.

Work

1x2s

2.

Weave the rope
in figure-eights.

End   Start

3.

Drive home
wedges under rope.

Single loop
shown for
clarity

I KNOW OF NO SIMPLER, cheaper, or more convenient method to
clamp up edge joints than the Spanish luthier's technique for joining guitar tops and backs. Though intended for thin wood, the technique is easily adaptable to any thickness, width, or length required. All
that is needed are several long wedges, a few 1x2s (longer than the
work is wide), and a length of ¼-in. rope.

When the work is ready to be glued, lay it on the 1x2s as shown in
step 1. Tie the rope to the right-hand stick and weave it over the work
and around both ends in a figure-eight. The diagram for step 2 shows
one figure-eight loop for clarity but several are necessary. Moving to
each 1x2 in turn, repeat weaving the figure-eights, tying off the rope
on the last stick.

Now insert the wedges under the middle of the figure-eights and drive them home with a mallet (see the illustration for step 3). This will apply clamping pressure without danger of the wood buckling and damage to the edge. Wax the wedges and 1x2s to prevent their being glued to the work by squeeze-out. The whole process is fast, but it's advisable to practice a few times to get the hang of the rope weaving.

—Douglass Peoples, *Arlington, Va.*

Assembly Squares

For assembling cabinets by myself, I have a set of assembly squares that I spring-clamp into corners to hold the parts perpendicular to each other. The squares act as a second pair of hands, holding the workpieces square and in alignment until I can spread the glue or drive home the screws. The webs are ¼-in. plywood, and the legs are 1x2s.

T.D. Culver, *Cleveland Heights, Ohio*

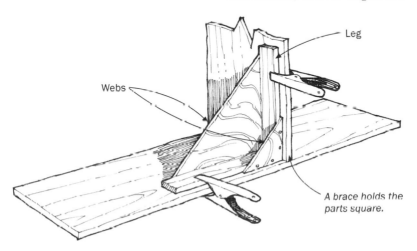

Leg

Webs

A brace holds the parts square.

Clamping with Metal Strapping

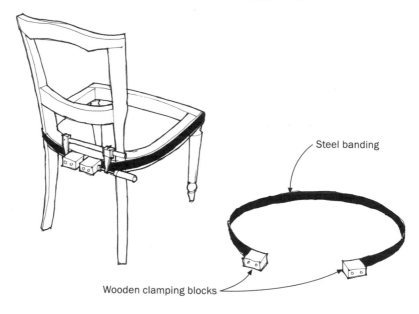

Steel banding

Wooden clamping blocks

WHEN I NEEDED A LARGE number of expensive webbing clamps for a run of chairs, I improvised this clamp. First retrieve a supply of metal strapping from the lumberyard scrap bin. Cut the strapping to the approximate length needed. Attach wooden blocks to each end with 3⁄16-in. bolts and nuts. Use a C-clamp or Quick-Grip clamp to tighten.

—CHRIS MARLEY, *Kingston, Jamaica*

Web-Clamp Work Holder

B ECAUSE OF THEIR SIZE and shape, the musical instruments I build are difficult to hold securely on the workbench for carving and routing. So I use this simple web-clamp system to hold instruments, or any other oddly shaped object, quite securely. Screw two or more web clamps to the apron of your workbench, as shown in the sketch below. When you need to secure a workpiece, grab the loose end of the web strap, thread it from below through one end of several pre-cut slots in your bench, then bring the strap up over the workpiece and back to the clamp. Now stick a fold of the web into the spool so that it is caught by the wrap around the tightening axle. Then tighten the clamp to secure the workpiece. If necessary, make a cradle, as shown, to hold the object.

—JEFFREY LEE GAYNOR, *Rootstown, Ohio*

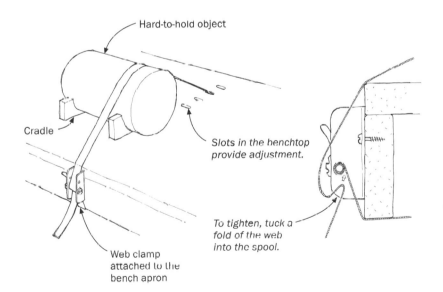

Hard-to-hold object

Cradle

Slots in the benchtop
provide adjustment.

To tighten, tuck a
fold of the web
into the spool.

Web clamp
attached to the
bench apron

Clamping Pedestal Table Legs

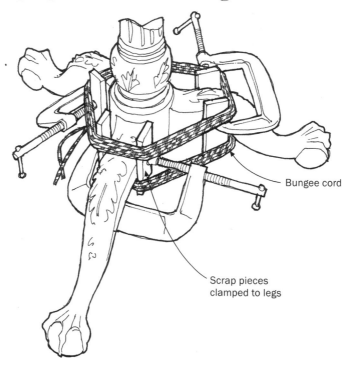

Bungee cord

Scrap pieces
clamped to legs

C LAMPING THE DOVETAILED LEGS of a pedestal table during glue-up is not easy—there is no place to put the clamps. On the first table I made, after a design by Franklin Gottshall, I left a square protrusion on the knee of the leg, per his suggestion, to provide a clamping perch. But the protrusion had to be removed later, leaving an awkward spot to be carved and shaped. Wiser the second time around, I used clamped scraps and a bungee cord, as shown in the sketch above. It worked perfectly, and it allowed me to finish carving the legs before gluing up the table.

—DR. THOMAS M. WHEELER, *Montgomery, Ala.*

Clamping Segmented Turning Blanks

WORM-SCREW HOSE CLAMPS make good, inexpensive gluing clamps for segmented turning blanks or other cylindrical gluing jobs. The clamps are available in hardware and automotive supply stores in sizes up to 6 in. in diameter. For larger diameters, simply screw two clamps together head-to-tail, or cut the band and install steel wire to extend the clamp's circumference. Marks and dents can be avoided by placing cardboard or wooden pads between the clamp and the work.

—W. L. CHESS, *Washington, Conn.*

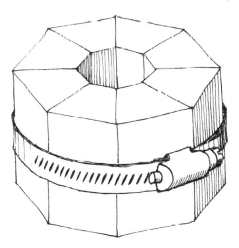

Assembling Staved Cylinders

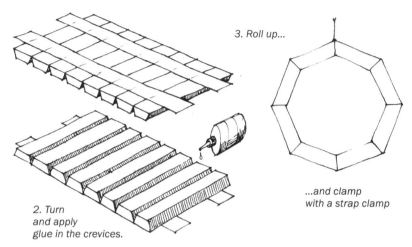

1. Apply plastic tape.

3. Roll up...

2. Turn and apply glue in the crevices.

...and clamp with a strap clamp

HERE'S A METHOD BASED on the principle of canvas-backed tambours that simplifies the assembly of staved cylinders. Lay the staves side by side on a flat surface and carefully align the ends. Apply rows of tape (I use 2-in.-wide plastic tape) to the outside surface. Turn the assembly over, apply glue to the stave edges, and roll up the cylinder. Apply a strap clamp to complete the job.

—POPE LAWRENCE, *Santa Fe, N.M.*

Clamp Perch for Round Tabletops

FEW THINGS PROVOKE LANGUAGE unbecoming a woodworker more than trying to clamp up a round tabletop. On a restoration project, I found myself having to rejoint and reglue the boards in two half-round top sections of a table. Cussin' didn't work, so I devised another scheme.

I scrounged up a nice straight-grained piece of ash about ¾ in. thick, and marked the center point on it and on the top of the curve of the outside table board. Then, rolling the stick along the circumference, I marked out perch points at appropriate clamping places—the sketch below shows one at each end, but you can make as many as you think you need—taking care to keep the flats parallel to the centerline of the table. Then I bandsawed the ash down to a springy ¼ in., leaving the perch spots as shown. To use, I bar-clamped the stick first in the middle, applying enough pressure so that it wouldn't slip. Then, working out from the middle, I bent the stick around the curve and gradually snugged up the clamps on each flat.

—JIM SMALL, *Newville, Pa.*

2. Bandsaw.

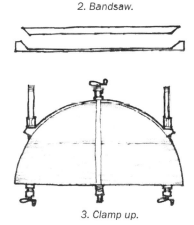

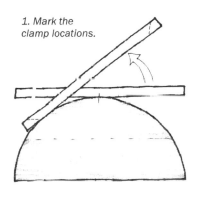

1. Mark the clamp locations.

3. Clamp up.

INDEX